SkillShift

Rethinking the way to lead your
Business Transformation.

Joel Velazquez
www.LearningSolutionsDelivery.com

SkillShift

RETHINKING THE WAY TO LEAD YOUR BUSINESS TRANSFORMATION.

Copyright © 2024 Joel Velazquez.

All rights reserved, including text, images, and charts. No part of this book may be used or reproduced by any means, graphic, electronic, or mechanical, including photocopying, recording, taping or by any information storage retrieval system without the written permission of the author except in the case of brief quotations embodied in critical articles and reviews.

iUniverse books may be ordered through booksellers or by contacting:

iUniverse
1663 Liberty Drive
Bloomington, IN 47403
www.iuniverse.com
844-349-9409

Because of the dynamic nature of the Internet, any web addresses or links contained in this book may have changed since publication and may no longer be valid. The views expressed in this work are solely those of the author and do not necessarily reflect the views of the publisher, and the publisher hereby disclaims any responsibility for them.

Any people depicted in stock imagery provided by Getty Images are models,
and such images are being used for illustrative purposes only.
Certain stock imagery © Getty Images.

ISBN: 978-1-6632-6804-4 (sc)
ISBN: 978-1-6632-6803-7 (e)

Library of Congress Control Number: 2024921949

Print information available on the last page.

iUniverse rev. date: 12/02/2024

Contents

Preface. How This Book Came to Be vii

Introduction. I Can Help You Lead Your Transformation Successfully ix

You Need a Leadership Framework. xiii

Setting the Stage: What's in It for You? xvii

It's all about SKILLS. xxi

    The Skill based model xxi

    We need 'M' people! xxiii

    Leadership is not about having all the answers. xxv

Part One. Your Transformation Starts Here! 1

    Step 1. The WHAT 3

    Step 2. The WHY 7

Part Two. Designing Your Transformation 11

    Step 3. The HOW 11

Part Three. The Foundation 17

    The Four Pillars for Doing the Right Things Right© 17

Part Four. Bringing It All Together. 123

    Primary Outcomes. 123

    Connecting the Dots: Turning Knowledge into Action 137

    Your Next Steps to Becoming a Skillful Leader 149

Conclusion. Elevate Your Leadership Game Now! 157

About the Author. 160

Index 163

Bibliography & References. 171

To Cristina, Danel, and Emilio—Thank you for trusting my lead and standing by me throughout this challenging journey...

Preface

How This Book Came to Be

"If you want to change the future, you must change what you're doing in the present."
— Mark Twain

Years ago, while working for Ford Motor Company in Latin America, I was deeply immersed in a transformative program focused on quality control. Our management team, responsible for different domains, collaborated closely, yet I observed a striking contrast in the outcomes achieved by the various business units. Leaders across manufacturing, supply chain, organizational development, and IT faced similar challenges, however their results varied significantly. This disparity led me to question why some leaders excel while others falter, despite facing comparable circumstances.

My journey continued at American Express, where I noticed the same pattern in a completely different industry. The contrasts in leadership outcomes mirrored those I had seen at Ford. Although I had limited access to the C-Suite at the time, I remained keenly focused on understanding what made certain approaches succeed and others fail.

Today, as an independent advisor in Canada, working with both public and private sector organizations undergoing major transformations, I've observed a similar theme. Despite facing similar odds, why do some executives thrive while others struggle? This question inspired me to create a versatile framework that can simplify even the most complex transformations, empowering leaders of all backgrounds to **leverage its insights** and achieve extraordinary results.

Introduction

I Can Help You Lead Your Transformation Successfully.

"Change before you have to."
— Jack Welch

Over the years, I've been a student of the game. A student of how transformation initiatives work, constantly analyzing what makes certain leaders successful while others falter under similar conditions. This underscored a crucial lesson—success in transformation isn't just about resources or circumstances; it's about leadership choices. This realization drove me to seek out frameworks and models that could offer practical solutions. However, many existing approaches were either overly complex or outdated, leading me to craft my own methodology.

This book will delve into the twists and turns of business transformation, with a particular focus on the Canadian public sector. Nevertheless, while these insights are tailored for a public sector context, they can easily be applied to any organization undergoing change in a competitive market. The private sector's lessons will come in future work, but for now, the spotlight is on how public sector leaders can navigate transformation effectively.

Where's Why it's Worth the Effort

It's easy to assume that transformation will happen naturally if you have good planning and the necessary resources in place. However, effective leadership is often the missing ingredient to determine success. This book explores the importance of focusing on leadership best practices when it comes to transformation and how this approach can have a significant impact driving positive outcomes.

Designed as a practical guide, this book draws on my three decades of experience, condensing the key insights of transformational leadership into a framework that is both accessible and adaptable. It's not about reinventing leadership but about leveraging proven models to thrive in today's challenging landscape.

In the following chapters, I will break down the key components of this framework, share real-world examples, and provide actionable insights to help you lead your transformation successfully. Together, we will rethink how leadership in transformation can—and should—be approached, equipping you with the tools to excel.

Transformational leadership often brings anxiety and frustration, emotions that can be daunting but manageable with the right strategies. My framework offers practical approaches that empower leaders to confidently navigate their organizations through transformation, ultimately guiding them toward success. By prioritizing leadership, we can unlock the full potential of transformation efforts and ensure meaningful change.

Think about this shortlist of challenges as a starter:

- **Talent and Skills Shortage:** Doubts about the availability of necessary talent and skills within the government can be overwhelming, especially for those newly appointed to leadership roles. The feeling of being underprepared for the monumental task ahead can be paralyzing.
- **Bureaucratic Frustration:** The complex bureaucracy and administrative processes within government agencies often act as significant barriers, slowing down transformative initiatives and leaving leaders frustrated and seeking a way out.

- **Political Backlash Fear:** The fear of political backlash and negative public perception looms large, particularly when implementing changes that address sensitive issues or face opposition from conflicting positions. These concerns can weigh heavily on leaders.
- **Budget Concerns:** Securing funding and resources for transformation initiatives is a persistent challenge. Government budgets are rigorously scrutinized, and obtaining necessary financial support amid competing demands is a substantial task.
- **Regulatory Uncertainty:** Concerns about compliance with existing regulatory frameworks can lead to legal challenges or delays, creating uncertainty around proposed transformations.
- **Data Security Concerns:** Ensuring the security of sensitive government data is critical. Any doubts or vulnerabilities in this area can generate significant anxiety.
- **Workforce Resistance:** Resistance within the government workforce, fueled by fears of job insecurity or unfamiliarity with new technologies, presents a considerable obstacle that needs to be addressed.
- **Interoperability Challenges:** The ability of different government agencies to integrate their systems and data is crucial for seamless transformation. Concerns about interoperability can hinder progress.
- **Balancing Political and Citizen-Centric Approaches:** Finding the right balance between political considerations and a commitment to citizen-centric solutions is a continuous challenge, raising doubts about whether the chosen approach is optimal.
- **Sustainability and Inclusivity Concerns:** Doubts about the long-term sustainability of transformation efforts and their benefits for all Canadians, particularly marginalized or underrepresented communities, highlight the need for truly inclusive and forward-thinking initiatives.

These challenges are common in transformation journeys, but each also presents an opportunity for growth and innovation. Let's explore how to turn these obstacles into steppingstones for success.

You Need a Leadership Framework.

"Leadership is the capacity to translate vision into reality."
— Warren Bennis

Regardless of your title or the size of the team you lead, as a leader or manager, you're likely facing complex challenges that require creative, effective solutions. If this resonates with you, you've found a valuable resource.

In today's fast-changing world, the need for transformative leadership has never been more urgent. Whether your organization is undergoing major change, your team is managing a demanding project, you're navigating a multifaceted challenge, or you've become a catalyst for innovation, this book is your guide. It provides the tools and strategies you need to lead with confidence and drive lasting success.

It's for those who've encountered the obstacles we all know too well, challenges such as:

- **Lack of Clarity and Direction**: Amid change, you struggle with uncertainty, unclear directives, and a lack of transparency from leadership. This confusion ripples through your teams.
- **Ineffective Collaboration and Communication**: Your teams are struggling to work together cohesively, and the idea of thinking beyond conventional solutions feels like a distant dream.
- **Resistance and Push-Back**: Employees or stakeholders are not fully onboard with your vision. Overcoming objections and addressing resistance has become an uphill battle.
- **Ineffective Change Management Strategies**: Past change initiatives have fallen short of their goals, leaving you searching for a new approach.
- **Measuring Progress and Success**: You're unsure how to gauge the progress and success of your change initiatives. Tangible results are the target, but you're not quite hitting the mark.

Perhaps you aspire to something like this:

- **Effective Problem-Solving:** You seek innovative and practical solutions for the intricate challenges you face.
- **Successful Change and Transformation:** Your organization is poised for significant change, and your goal is to guide it through a seamless and successful transition.
- **Effective Collaboration and Teamwork:** You're driven to foster a culture of innovation, creativity, and collaboration within your team.
- **Skill Development and Growth:** Acquiring the skills and knowledge required to tackle your challenges head-on is your priority.
- **Accountability and Feedback:** You want to ensure that you're on the right path, receiving guidance and feedback as you navigate the transformation journey.

If any of these aspirations or challenges resonate with you, **then this is my bold promise:**

This book is a path to seamlessly develop the critical skills and knowledge needed for successful change management and business transformation, all without the burdensome expense and time investment that often accompanies traditional training methods, even if you're already overwhelmed by your current workload.

What follows in the pages ahead represents the culmination of a lifetime of experiences and years of relentless thinking and research. Together, we will explore highly effective tactics that will redefine your approach to leadership.

As we journey through the chapters of this book, I will unveil my signature framework—the C.H.A.N.G.E. Framework for Doing the Right Things Right© — it offers a systematic, step-by-step approach to business transformation. This framework is part of an overarching model consisting of 3 Steps and 4 Pillars, which will serve as a compass that I am sure will align with your hopes as it outlines a clear path to leading a transformation initiative.

To get the most out of this book, I encourage you to read it from start to finish. While it's an accessible read, it's packed with insights drawn from a range of trusted sources, including proven strategies from leading experts. My role has been to distill these insights into a clear, actionable formula that empowers you throughout your transformation journey. By the time you finish, you'll have a complete blueprint to tackle your transformation challenges effectively.

What follows is a four-part framework designed to transform the way you approach change—providing you with a fresh perspective that's sure to deliver better outcomes.

So let's get started!

Setting the Stage: What's in It for You?

"Leadership and learning are indispensable to each other."
— John F. Kennedy

I consider myself a knowledge broker, someone who bridges the gap between information and its practical application, helping others turn knowledge into real results. My transition from employee to knowledge broker started during my work with multinational corporations, where exposure to different countries, industries, and cultures uniquely shaped my growth.

Looking back, much of my progress came through trial and error. Fueled by a desire to improve, I developed my "Secret Sauce"—a set of eight mindsets refined through personal experience and introspection. Over time, I realized these principles aligned with established models I encountered through advanced courses and research. Their proven effectiveness inspired me to share them, giving credit where due.

My goal is to simplify these models into a practical blueprint, helping others navigate their challenges more effectively. By adopting these mindsets, readers can turn theories into practical strategies, accelerating both personal and professional growth. The hard work has been done—I've taken complex concepts and distilled them into actionable insights, offering a roadmap to avoid common pitfalls and achieve greater success.

Had I known these mindsets and frameworks earlier in my career, I would have achieved significant success much sooner. Although I didn't have a coach to guide me then, I am here now to offer you that support and guidance.

But there's a CATCH!

This guide is for those who see knowledge as a lifelong journey, value learning from others, and are committed to continuous growth and challenging the norm. If that resonates with you, you're in the right place. The approach here is designed to empower, not prescribe. My role is to provide the tools and insights you need to shape your own path.

Imagine having a framework that serves as a dependable compass, where mastering a few key principles can drive most of your success. That's the advantage I offer. But to fully benefit, you need to actively engage and apply what you learn.

Think of this as the start of your journey—an effective tool ready for you to use. Your success will depend on the effort and commitment you make. The potential is significant, but it's your active participation that will unlock it.

Ultimately, this framework is here to guide and support your growth, but its real power comes from the energy you invest. Embrace the challenge, and you'll discover it as a valuable asset in achieving your goals.

Key Takeaways.

Here are the key takeaways from this chapter, highlighting the essential insights and strategies to help you lead successful transformations:

- **Differing Transformation Outcomes:** Observations from various industries showed that the success of transformative initiatives differed greatly, even under similar conditions, depending on the leadership quality.

- **Simplified Leadership Framework:** Emphasized the importance of creating an easy-to-use, flexible framework for business transformations, grounded in practical experience and established models.

- **From Knowledge to Action:** This framework transforms theoretical concepts into tangible results

- **Addressing Common Leadership Challenges:** Leaders frequently encountered issues like talent shortages, bureaucratic obstacles political pressures, and resistance to change, which were effectively managed with appropriate strategies.

- **Empowerment through Knowledge:** The C.H.A.N.G.E.© Framework offers a structured approach to transformation, integrating insights from established theories and real-world experiences to equip leaders with the tools they need.

- **Active Engagement Required:** The effectiveness of the framework depends on the reader's proactive engagement and willingness to apply the provided insights thoughtfully in their own context.

It's all about SKILLS.

"The more you learn, the more you earn."
— Warren Buffett

Picture this: two individuals tackling the same task. One brings years of experience and extensive knowledge, while the other excels with a refined set of skills. Which one is more likely to succeed?

I firmly believe that skills are the key to standing out. While knowledge and experience are undeniably valuable, it's the adept application of skills that truly drives success. Imagine having a toolbox where each tool represents a skill, such as communication, problem-solving, or adaptability. The real strength lies in knowing how to use each tool effectively, selecting the right one for each challenge, and applying it precisely when needed.

In a rapidly changing world, adaptability and agility—both rooted in skill—become crucial. Success isn't about having all the answers but about having the skills to navigate uncertainties, innovate swiftly, and seize new opportunities. Skills empower you to face evolving challenges and leverage opportunities in a dynamic landscape.

Ultimately, in leadership and beyond, it's not just about what you know but how skillfully you apply it. Embrace the power of skills, and you'll find yourself better equipped to handle the complexities of any situation.

The Skill based model.

To illustrate the importance of skills in leadership, consider the Skills Model developed by American organizational psychologists Michael D. Mumford, Stephen J. Zaccaro, and Francis D. Harding in 2000[1]. This model provides a practical framework for understanding effective leadership through skills. It emphasizes that successful leaders are distinguished by their **problem-solving abilities**, **social judgment**, and **relevant knowledge**. Problem-solving skills allow leaders to navigate complex situations and make informed decisions. Social judgment skills help leaders manage relationships and influence others effectively. Knowledge ensures leaders have the expertise needed to understand and address organizational challenges.

Additionally, the social psychologist Robert L. Katz, from the University of Chicago, in his work dating back to 1955[2] introduced a three-skill approach to management, which remains relevant to this day. Katz highlighted the importance of **technical**, **human**, and **conceptual skills**. Technical skills involve specialized knowledge, human skills focus on interpersonal relations, and conceptual skills relate to strategic thinking. Katz's framework shows that **as leaders ascend in the organizational structure, the importance of these skills shifts.** Lower-level managers rely more on technical and interpersonal skills, while higher-level managers need a balance of all three, with an increasing focus on conceptual thinking.

These models collectively underscore that effective leadership hinges on skill development rather than just theoretical knowledge. By focusing on building and applying skills in problem-solving, interpersonal relations, and strategic thinking, leaders can better navigate the complexities of their roles and drive positive outcomes.

In essence, the shift towards skill-focused leadership highlights the need for continuous learning and practical application. Leaders who prioritize and develop these key skills are better equipped to handle the dynamic challenges and opportunities in today's organizational contexts.

A shortcut to success. Knowledge vs. Experience

In Leadership Skills for a Changing World (2000)[3], another of Michael D. Mumford's relevant research, he argues that effective leadership today hinges more on skill refinement than on knowledge or experience alone. His **SAGE model—Self-confidence**, **Agility**, **Grit**, **Engagement**, and **Empathy—** captures this idea, emphasizing that these core attributes are crucial for navigating modern business challenges.

Self-confidence in this model goes beyond self-assurance; it's about inspiring trust and confidence in others. Agility involves being proactive and responsive to changes, not just adapting but anticipating and leading through dynamic shifts. Grit represents the determination and resilience needed to persist through difficulties and stay focused on goals.

Mumford also underscores the significance of Engagement and Empathy. Engagement involves actively collaborating and building strong teams to drive positive change, while Empathy emphasizes understanding and valuing diverse perspectives to foster innovation.

Overall, the SAGE model illustrates that mastering these skills is vital for effective leadership, especially in the complex and evolving landscape of government work. By focusing on developing these attributes, leaders can enhance their effectiveness and successfully navigate the challenges they face.

We need 'M' people!

So, what type of person are you?

Tim Brown of IDEO[4] coined the term "T-shaped people" to describe individuals who combine deep expertise in a specific area (the vertical stroke of the T) with a broad range of experiences and skills (the horizontal stroke). This blend makes them highly adaptable and effective in various roles within a team. However, other profiles like "M-shaped," "I-shaped," "P-shaped," and "E-shaped" people also offer unique strengths.

"M-shaped people" have expertise in multiple fields, allowing them to tackle diverse challenges and contribute flexibly to various projects. For instance, Benjamin Franklin's prowess in science, politics, and diplomacy exemplifies the M-shaped profile, demonstrating versatility and broad capabilities.

"I-shaped people" focus on deep specialization in one area, offering invaluable insights but often lacking the breadth of other profiles. Albert Einstein's groundbreaking work in theoretical physics is a prime example, showcasing the depth of knowledge typical of I-shaped individuals.

"Π-shaped people" (inspired by the Greek letter Pi) combine broad foundational knowledge with multiple deep specialties. They balance the adaptability of T-shaped individuals with the diverse expertise of M-shaped ones. Marie Curie, excelling across scientific disciplines, embodies this profile, blending wide-ranging skills with profound expertise.

"E-shaped people" emphasize experience, expertise, exploration, and execution, excelling in turning ideas into tangible outcomes. Leonardo da Vinci's achievements in art, engineering, and anatomy reflect the E-shaped profile's focus on practical application and innovation.

By understanding these profiles, you can identify your strengths and areas for growth, enabling you to leverage your unique capabilities in a way that enhances your effectiveness and adaptability in any role. Embrace the type that resonates with you, and you'll be better positioned to navigate the complexities of your professional landscape.

Here's a table summarizing the five letters with their corresponding descriptions and examples [5]

Letter	Description	Example
T	Specialized skill set with broader experiences	Tim Berners-Lee
M	Multiple specialties, offering versatility	Benjamin Franklin
I	Deep expertise in a specific area	Albert Einstein
Π or Pi	Combination of breadth and multiple specialties	Marie Curie
E	Emphasis on experience, exploration, execution	Leonardo da Vinci

When it comes to learning new skills, understanding the unique strengths of different skill profiles is crucial. Among these, "E-shaped people" and "M-shaped people" stand out as excellent options for those looking to re-skill or up-skill. Both profiles offer distinct advantages, and determining which is more suitable depends on individual preferences, the nature of the work, and specific goals.

The M-shaped profile provides versatility and flexibility, allowing individuals to draw on expertise from multiple specialties. This breadth enables M-shaped individuals to contribute effectively to diverse projects and tackle complex challenges, making them particularly valuable in dynamic environments where adaptability is key.

In contrast, the E-shaped profile emphasizes experience, expertise, exploration, and execution, focusing on turning ideas into reality. E-shaped individuals excel at hands-on problem-solving and innovation, making them indispensable for driving tangible results and bringing concepts to fruition.

Ultimately, the choice between these profiles should align with the specific context and requirements of the situation. In specialized fields where deep expertise is essential, an M-shaped profile may be more beneficial. However, in fast-paced, innovative settings where rapid execution is crucial, an E-shaped profile could provide a greater advantage.

Recognizing that both profiles have valuable contributions encourages collaboration within teams. By leveraging the strengths of diverse skill sets, organizations can achieve more comprehensive and effective outcomes. Rather than debating which profile is superior, it's more beneficial to appreciate the unique attributes each brings and strive for a balanced combination within teams.

So, which profile resonates with you? Are you more aligned with the versatile, multi-specialty approach of the M-shaped individual, or do you lean towards the practical, execution-focused mindset of the E-shaped individual? Identifying your profile enables you to leverage your strengths and make a meaningful contribution toward achieving your goals.

Leadership is not about having all the answers.

Leadership today is less about having all the answers and more about guiding teams through uncertainty with humility and emotional intelligence. Effective leaders understand that they don't need to know everything; instead, they excel by asking the right questions and valuing diverse perspectives. Tim Brown from IDEO[6] highlights this shift, emphasizing that leadership involves facilitating creativity and innovation rather than dictating solutions. By fostering an environment where curiosity and open dialogue are encouraged, leaders can tap into their teams' full potential.

Similarly, Robert S. Kaplan[7] stresses the importance of seeking feedback and maintaining open communication channels. M-shaped individuals, with their broad range of skills and experience, are adept at cultivating such environments. They leverage their versatility to actively seek diverse feedback and adapt their strategies accordingly. This approach not only drives innovation but also reinforces the need for leaders to remain humble and receptive to input from all team members, regardless of their rank.

In essence, the connection between both articles and the concept of M-shaped people reviewed earlier, lies in the emphasis on skills such as curiosity, versatility, communication, and relationship-building in driving effective leadership and professional development. Central to this modern approach is the role of emotional intelligence. Effective leaders understand that they don't have all the answers and are comfortable acknowledging this. Embracing humility and valuing input from all team members—regardless of their position—enhances decision-making and fosters a collaborative culture. By integrating skills, emotional intelligence, and a commitment to continuous learning, leaders can more effectively navigate today's dynamic work environments, increasing their chances of success.

Key Takeaways.

The journey to exceptional leadership is less about accumulating knowledge and more about mastering essential skills. Let's distill the core insights from our exploration:

- Success is driven more by skills than by knowledge and experience.
- Effective leadership hinges on a combination of problem-solving, social judgment, and relevant knowledge.
- Adaptability, agility, and emotional intelligence are essential for modern leadership.
- M-shaped and E-shaped individuals offer unique strengths, with a balance of both being optimal for team success.
- Successful leaders focus on building and applying skills, seeking feedback, and fostering a collaborative environment.

Part One. Your Transformation Starts Here!

"Efficiency is doing things right; effectiveness is doing the right things."
— Henry Ford

Introducing the C.H.A.N.G.E. Framework for Doing the Right Things Right©

Welcome to the beginning of your transformation journey. In the following pages, we'll delve into practical strategies to enhance and evolve your public service organization. Transformation is not a one-time event but a continuous process of improvement and innovation, requiring both the right tools and the right mindset.

To simplify this journey, I've structured a comprehensive framework that consists of **three key steps**, **four foundational pillars**, and **three essential takeaways**.

- The **three steps** will address the what, the why, and the how of your transformation, providing a clear and comprehensive understanding of each phase.
- The **four foundational pillars** will provide a solid base upon which you can build and sustain your transformation efforts, ensuring that every aspect of your strategy is grounded in solid principles.
- The **three essential takeaways** will serve as practical templates, helping you articulate and implement your strategies effectively. These takeaways are crafted to be actionable and adaptable, allowing you to tailor them to your specific needs and challenges.

This systematic approach is intended to ensure that you focus on the right actions, follow best practices, and achieve meaningful results in a structured and efficient manner.

Let's dive in and uncover the practical methods to unlock your organization's full potential. As they say, a picture is worth a thousand words—so let's review Exhibit #1 below, and we'll break down its elements one at a time.

Exhibit #1

Step 1. The WHAT

Define your Mission Possible:

A clearly defined mission from the start streamlines the entire process, making it easier to align efforts with core objectives and prioritize impactful projects. Let's begin by outlining our goal—our Mission Possible.

Think back to the classic TV series "Mission: Impossible." In those episodes, a mysterious package would arrive, detailing the mission's objectives and the necessary actions to prevent disaster. The key was having a clear goal and a compelling reason to succeed; without this clarity, the mission would falter.

In business transformation, we must adopt a similar mindset. Before diving into the details of achieving our goals, we need to clearly define our Mission Possible—**what we aim to accomplish** and **what we want to avoid**. By answering these questions, we establish a strong foundation for our journey.

With a clear understanding of our goals, we can effectively tackle challenges and navigate the path to successful transformation. By defining our Mission Possible, we ensure that all efforts align with our core objectives, making it simpler to prioritize impactful projects and achieve meaningful results.

<u>Imagine this scenario:</u>

During a digital transformation initiative to modernize service delivery systems within the Federal Government of Canada, your client established a clear mission: enhancing citizen experience through streamlined access to government services while ensuring data security and privacy. This focused approach yielded remarkable results. By aligning their efforts with this mission, the client prioritized projects that directly enhanced citizen experience. They introduced user-friendly digital platforms—like online forms, portals, and mobile apps—that made government services more accessible. This not only simplified processes but also reduced wait times, leading to greater satisfaction among citizens.

By emphasizing data security and privacy, the client not only improved citizen experience but also ensured compliance with regulations and protected sensitive information. Implementing robust cybersecurity measures across all digital channels safeguarded personal data, building trust in government services.

With a clearly defined Mission Possible, the client effectively allocated resources. Budgets were directed toward initiatives that aligned with their mission, maximizing investment impact and delivering tangible results while adhering to budget constraints. This approach exemplified fiscal responsibility and effective resource management.

The results were clear: enhanced citizen experience, strengthened data security, and optimized resource allocation positioned the client as a leader in digital government services.

In contrast, without a clearly defined Mission Possible, the initiative could have encountered significant challenges. Misaligned efforts may have resulted in scattered priorities, diverting resources to projects that did not directly improve the citizen experience. This could have led to disjointed and inefficient digital platforms, frustrating users due to a lack of integration and usability.

Citizens might have continued to face long wait times and cumbersome processes, undermining the initiative's goal of streamlining access to government services. Neglecting user-friendly design could have made digital services less accessible, worsening existing barriers and diminishing overall satisfaction.

Moreover, insufficient attention to data security and privacy could have left sensitive information vulnerable to breaches. Weak cybersecurity measures might have resulted in data leaks, eroding public trust in the government's ability to protect personal information, leading to serious legal and reputational repercussions, including fines for non-compliance with regulations and damage to government credibility.

In summary, without a clear Mission Possible, the transformation effort could have resulted in inefficient resource use, ineffective digital solutions, increased citizen dissatisfaction, and compromised data security. This misalignment would not only hinder the initiative's success but also expose the government to significant operational and legal risks.

The next critical step is to clearly define what our next steps are. And to do this we must identify specific, measurable actions that will move us closer to our goals. Then we must ask ourselves what our value proposition is. How to clearly articulate the distinct benefits and unique offerings that achieving our mission will bring, providing a guiding principle to align our organization toward common objectives.

In the public service context, the value proposition focuses on serving the public and addressing community needs rather than competing with others. It highlights the distinct advantages stakeholders—citizens and government agencies—will experience because of our initiatives. Our value proposition will:

- **Clarify Our Impact:** Define how our services enhance community well-being and address public concerns.
- **Strengthen Stakeholder Engagement:** Emphasize the value our initiatives bring to the public and government partners.
- **Guide Decision-Making:** Provide a framework for prioritizing actions and resources based on the public value we aim to deliver.

By establishing a compelling value proposition, we create a clear, unified direction for public service efforts, enhance our strategic focus on community impact, and reinforce our commitment to delivering meaningful outcomes for the public.

The most effective approach is to follow this format:

> For [target user], who [user need], [our Value Prop] solves/provides/helps [benefit]

To provide context, in the case of my consulting company, this would be my value proposition:

> For the **GoC Executive**, who **needs expert advice on how to lead** its organizational business transformation, SkillShift Coaching can **help leverage best practices, operationalize processes, and adopt tools** that **lead to effective and efficient implementation** of key initiatives..

If that makes sense to you, now go ahead and draft your own version, the one that best aligns with your challenge at hand.

Key Takeaways.

The next table summarizes our imaginary scenario in terms of Step #1, the WHAT:

Aspect	Happy Path	Failure Path (Actual Results)
Define Your **Mission Possible**	Establish a **specific, well-articulated goal** for the transformation initiative to ensure alignment and focus.	Proceed **without a clear goal**, leading to scattered priorities and misalignment.
What Do You **Want to Achieve?**	Enhancing citizen experience through **streamlined access** to services and robust data security.	Disjointed digital platforms that **fail to improve citizen experience**, with ineffective data security measures.
What Do You **Want to Avoid?**	**Avoid inefficient use of resources**, misaligned projects, and inadequate data protection.	Avoid misallocation of resources, **user frustration, and vulnerabilities** in data security.
What are your **Next Steps** & **Value Proposition?**	Deliver user-friendly digital services that are secure and compliant, enhancing public trust and satisfaction.	**Suboptimal digital solutions** that frustrate users and risk data breaches, undermining public trust.

Potential Outcomes:	• **Focus on Data Security and Privacy**: Apply robust cybersecurity measures and ensure compliance with regulatory requirements to protect sensitive information. • **Ensure Integration and Efficiency:** Develop cohesive, integrated systems that streamline processes and reduce wait times for users.	• **Ignore Data Security and Privacy:** Overlook cybersecurity, leading to potential data breaches and loss of public trust. • **Disjointed Systems:** Create fragmented systems that hinder efficiency, increase wait times, and complicate processes.

Step 2. The WHY

To lead an effective business transformation, understanding our WHY is crucial. This vision, purpose, and focus on human impact drive meaningful actions. By visualizing the end goal, recognizing the stakes involved, and prioritizing people, leaders can forge a future defined by purpose and success.

A clear and compelling vision serves as the cornerstone of successful transformation. Just as a captain charts a course, leaders must envision the finish line before embarking on the journey. This clarity inspires passion and aligns teams toward a shared goal.

Transformation transcends new technology or processes; it reshapes the organization's trajectory and impact. By grasping the implications of transformation, leaders can effectively communicate its importance, inspire commitment, and instill a sense of urgency. Whether the aim is innovation, growth, or addressing societal challenges, a well-executed transformation ensures long-term success and relevance.

To truly harness the power of transformation, leaders should consider two essential questions:

- Why do people need this to happen?
- Why is it a game changer in people's lives?

By stepping into the shoes of others and looking beyond their own perspectives, leaders gain valuable insights into the human impact of transformation.

Transformation reaches far beyond boardrooms and balance sheets; it significantly affects people's lives. It's not just about bottom-line results; it's about empowering individuals, enriching communities, and creating meaningful change. Transformation offers hope for a better future, fostering growth, fulfillment, and prosperity for the organization and all its contributors. By recognizing and articulating the human dimension of transformation, leaders can galvanize support and cultivate a culture of resilience and adaptability in the face of uncertainty.

Key Takeaways.

Reflecting on our hypothetical case from the previous section, the following table summarizes the implications related to Step #2, **the WHY**:

Aspect	Happy Path:	Failure Path:
Foresee a clear **VISION** of the **FINISH LINE**	Clearly defined vision **guides all efforts** toward enhancing citizen experience, data security, and efficiency.	Unclear vision leads to **scattered priorities**, wasted resources, and suboptimal outcomes.
Why **people need this to happen?**	Citizens need **streamlined, secure access** to government services to save time, reduce frustration, and protect personal information.	Citizens suffer from long wait times, complex processes, and data breaches, **eroding trust in government**.

Why it's **a game changer** in people's lives?	A clear vision **empowers citizens** to interact efficiently with government, improving their quality of life and fostering trust in government institutions.	Without a clear vision, **citizens experience frustration**, inconvenience, and a sense of vulnerability, damaging their perception of government.
Potential Outcomes:	• **Enhanced Public Satisfaction:** Citizens experience smoother, more efficient interactions with government services, leading to increased trust and satisfaction with the federal government. • **Strengthened Data Security:** Robust cybersecurity measures prevent data breaches and ensure compliance with regulations, protecting sensitive information and avoiding legal repercussions.	• **Increased Public Frustration:** Disjointed services and inefficient processes frustrate citizens, leading to decreased trust and satisfaction with government services. • **Data Security Breaches:** Weak cybersecurity measures result in data breaches, exposing personal information and leading to potential legal and reputational damage.

Part Two. Designing Your Transformation

"Success lies in how you approach the journey, not just the destination."
— Unknown

Step 3. The HOW

The third logical step after defining the **What** and the **Why** is to determine **How** to achieve our goals. To address this, let's consider a structured approach: a six-step process I've named C.H.A.N.G.E., which is part of the broader C.H.A.N.G.E. framework© mentioned earlier. This process provides a clear method within a comprehensive framework.

The C.H.A.N.G.E.© process emerged from my observations of recurring challenges across various organizations. I identified a sequence of essential steps that, when strategically followed, significantly enhance the likelihood of successful transformation. Recognizing these common pitfalls allowed me to create a systematic approach that is adaptable to each client's unique needs.

For illustration, refer to Exhibit #2 below. The process begins with Clarifying Goals, establishing a clear vision of what we want to achieve. Next, we assess the current situation to identify challenges and opportunities. The Harnessing Resources step involves securing both tangible assets and the crucial intangible support of stakeholders. Since successful transformations depend on widespread backing, gathering support and mobilizing resources is vital to building a robust network.

The Analyzing Gaps step focuses on understanding the disparities between the current state and the desired outcome. Conducting a thorough gap analysis is central to successful transformations, as it highlights the distance to our goals. The subsequent steps—Navigating Obstacles, Generating Solutions, and Evaluating Progress—reflect the dynamic nature of change initiatives. Change is not a straight path but a flexible journey that requires navigating obstacles, developing innovative solutions, and continuously assessing progress.

So, why is it called C.H.A.N.G.E.©? The acronym encapsulates the essence of transformation by breaking down key steps and reminding everyone that change is an ongoing process. The C.H.A.N.G.E.© framework represents the core principles of successful change management, grounded in real-world experiences.

Additionally, C.H.A.N.G.E.© embodies effective leadership by emphasizing the importance of doing the right things and executing them correctly. It aligns vision with action, underscores ethical decision-making, and ensures precise implementation. Like a compass guiding you to your North Star, C.H.A.N.G.E.© empowers leaders to make choices and take actions that are effective and in harmony with their vision and values.

Exhibit #2

So, what exactly does the C.H.A.N.G.E. Process© do?

(C) Clarifying Goals:

First, it's about taking stock of where you are and where you want to go. Assess the current landscape, spot challenges, and unveil opportunities. Then, set your sights on clear goals.

(H) Harnessing Resources:

Next, gather your crew and gather your resources. Identify the support you need, mobilize your assets, and build a network that's got your back every step of the way.

(A) Analyzing Gaps:

Now, let's bridge the divide. Identify any gaps between where you are and where you want to be. Dive deep into gap analysis to understand the distance to your goals.

(N) Navigating Obstacles:

Rough waters ahead? Fear not—this step is all about charting a course through the challenges. Face obstacles head-on, develop strategies, and navigate your ship towards success.

(G) Generating Solutions:

Time to get creative! Innovate for change, brainstorm bold solutions, and set sail with effective strategies to implement your vision.

(E) Evaluating Progress:

As you journey forward, keep an eye on the horizon. Monitor your transformation, evaluate your progress regularly, and adapt your course for successful outcomes.

| Bottom Line | This framework is designed to ignite your potential and provide a proven roadmap. The C.H.A.N.G.E.© Process, which I have successfully applied in numerous real-world situations, will help you integrate your skills and experience. It will empower you to lead change with purpose, excellence, and confidence. |

Consulting Case Study #1. Implementing the C.H.A.N.G.E. Process©:

A couple of years ago, I partnered with a provincial government entity undergoing a substantial technological and organizational transformation. While I can't disclose specific details to maintain confidentiality, the initial situation posed significant challenges. The organization struggled with unclear goals, leading to uncertainty about its direction. An outdated technological infrastructure caused inefficiencies, while a culture resistant to change and siloed departments resulted in communication breakdowns and widespread employee confusion.

Introducing the C.H.A.N.G.E.© Process yielded immediate improvements. The framework's simplicity and clarity were embraced, allowing us to focus on **Setting Clear Transformation Goals** (Clarifying Goals). This straightforward approach united both leadership and employees around a common objective. With goals defined, we turned our attention to **Harnessing Resources**. By engaging leaders and influencers, we built a cross-functional team that rallied support for the initiative.

The **Analyzing Gaps** phase identified discrepancies in technology, culture, and skills. The team recognized the challenge and grasped the gap between the current state and desired goals. During the **Navigating Obstacles** phase, we transformed resistance into acceptance through targeted strategies that emphasized incremental change and agile methodologies.

In the **Generating Solutions** phase, intensive brainstorming sessions sparked practical innovations. The organization not only acknowledged the necessity for change but actively participated in implementing effective solutions. Continuous evaluation became ingrained in the culture, with a robust system for regular **Progress Evaluation**.

The outcome? A once-confused organization emerged as an efficient entity with a clear path forward. Implementing the C.H.A.N.G.E.© Process not only streamlined my work but also empowered the client to independently identify and tackle challenges beyond the immediate transformation. This case study illustrates the transformative power of the C.H.A.N.G.E.© Process in driving successful and sustainable change. By embracing this framework, this organization was able to navigate its challenges, foster collaboration, and achieve meaningful, long-lasting outcomes within its transformation journey.

Key Takeaways.

Exceptional leadership requires a structured approach to complex change, rooted in clarity, resourcefulness, analysis, action, and evaluation. Let's recap our key findings:

- The C.H.A.N.G.E.© Process offers a systematic approach to transformation, stressing the importance of setting clear goals and resource mobilization.
- It breaks down the transformation process into six actionable steps, providing a clear roadmap for leaders to follow.
- Implementing the process involves setting a clear vision, assessing current challenges, harnessing support, and navigating obstacles with creativity

Part Three. The Foundation

"The mind is everything. What you think you become."
— Buddha

The Four Pillars for Doing the Right Things Right©

Building success from the ground up

As we mentioned in Part 1, in addition to the three steps (the What, the Why and the How), we have four foundational pillars, and three essential takeaways. Let's refer to Exhibit #3 for an easier explanation and look closely at each piece at a time:

Exhibit #3

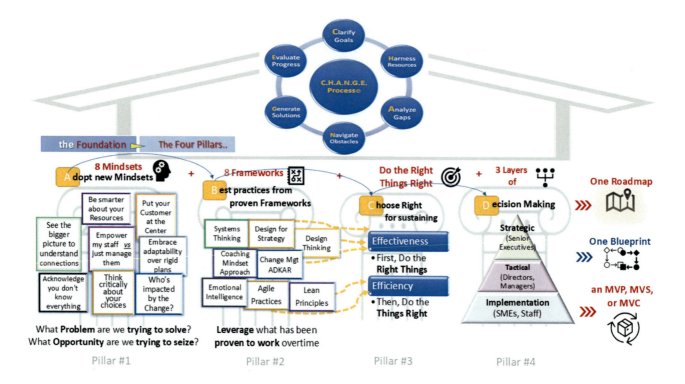

Pillar 1. Adopt New Mindsets.

What problem are we trying to solve? What opportunity are we trying to seize?

Responses to these questions can vary significantly based on individual perspectives and understanding. Some individuals articulate clear, focused explanations that break down issues into manageable parts, while others may struggle with ambiguity, offering vague or uncertain descriptions. Biases and assumptions can distort these responses, masking the true nature of the problem. Furthermore, diverse stakeholder perspectives can complicate our understanding of the problem's scope and implications.

Regardless of the answers we receive, it's essential to navigate common pitfalls during the problem-definition process. Clearly defined problem statements are crucial; vague descriptions can lead to confusion and misdirection. By focusing on symptoms rather than root causes, we risk developing solutions that fail to address the core issues. Overcomplicating the problem can make it seem more daunting and hinder progress, while ignoring stakeholder input and rushing through the process may result in incomplete definitions and ineffective solutions.

Biases and assumptions can cloud judgment, impeding impartial analysis. Additionally, a lack of alignment among team members and the tendency to either oversimplify or overcomplicate issues can exacerbate these challenges. To overcome these obstacles, it's vital to avoid prematurely assuming solutions and to actively involve key stakeholders in defining the problem. Addressing framing biases, ensuring access to sufficient data, maintaining a broad focus, and regularly reevaluating the problem are essential steps. Clear communication is also key; avoiding ambiguous language or jargon fosters a shared understanding among team members and enhances problem-solving efforts.

By following these guidelines, we can effectively define the problem and seize opportunities for meaningful solutions.

Put your Customer at the Center. Think like a Designer

Inspired by my older sister, an industrial designer, I was always fascinated by her creative approach to challenges. Her ability to merge beauty and functionality through a unique perspective made me consider how I could incorporate a similar mindset into my own work. Observing these challenges repeatedly, I sought a different approach. I realized the need to analyze problems from a fresh perspective—one that would allow me to grasp the full scope of issues and uncover innovative solutions. I committed to thinking like a designer, exploring various potential solutions and validating them through collaboration and feedback.

By embracing this mindset, I tackled challenges with creativity, exploration, and iteration. This approach enabled me to move beyond surface-level symptoms and uncover the underlying causes of problems. I adopted prototyping and iterative testing, gathering feedback from stakeholders to refine and enhance solutions.

Thinking like a designer also meant prioritizing empathy and understanding the needs and perspectives of those affected by the problem. I engaged in active listening and open communication to ensure diverse viewpoints were considered and fostered a collaborative environment where innovative ideas could thrive.

Additionally, I emphasized flexibility and adaptability, recognizing that problem definitions might evolve as new information emerged. This iterative process helped me stay responsive to changes and continually improve solutions.

Ultimately, adopting a designer's mindset transformed my approach to problem-solving. It empowered me to think creatively, engage stakeholders meaningfully, and navigate the complexities of problem definition with a clearer, more effective strategy.

Design Process Intent

With all this in mind, I came up with a simple process that I will describe below. Let's look at the following visual to keep things simple.

Exhibit #4

Design process intent:
    Explore multiple options and let others validate them..

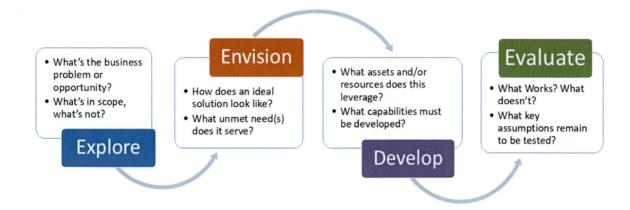

My design process begins with **Explore**, where I focus on understanding the business problem or opportunity at hand. This phase involves determining what is within scope and what is not, establishing a clear boundary for the project.

In the **Envision** stage, I envision how an ideal solution would look and identify the unmet needs it should address. This step is crucial for shaping the direction of the design and ensuring that the solution aligns with business goals.

Moving to the **Develop** phase, I gauge the assets and resources available and determine the capabilities that need to be developed. This involves leveraging existing resources and planning for any new skills or tools required to implement the solution effectively.

Finally, in the **Evaluate** stage, I assess what works and what doesn't, identifying key assumptions that remain to be tested. This iterative approach allows for ongoing refinement and validation of the solution, ensuring it meets the defined needs and achieves the desired outcomes.

Bottom Line:

This design process serves as a strategic framework that effectively transforms business challenges into innovative solutions. By systematically exploring problem domains, envisioning optimal outcomes, developing essential capabilities, and rigorously evaluating results, organizations can create impactful solutions that propel business growth and ensure long-term success. Leveraging this iterative approach allows for continuous improvement and adaptability, enabling teams to respond effectively to evolving challenges and opportunities.

Adopt new mindsets.

Over time, this straightforward process yielded impressive results. It provided a clear structure for engaging with clients, significantly reducing guesswork and enhancing understanding of their environments. This shift in perspective—viewing challenges through a new lens—was a transformative moment for me.

By centering my problem-solving efforts around the customer, I significantly increased the likelihood that my solutions would align with their needs and preferences. Focusing on their pain points, expectations, and desires allowed me to create solutions that were not only effective but also resonated with a broader audience. While this may seem obvious today, these insights emerged from my experiences two decades ago, laying the groundwork for my approach. We will explore this further in the next chapter.

Reflecting on the success I achieved by adopting this new mindset, I began to wonder how I could better serve my clients by continually evolving my approach to make our collaborations even more effective. I began to wonder:

- How could I help them optimize their resources—time, materials, and finances?
- How could I help them empower their staff in a way that aligns their roles with their evolving goals versus just managing them?
- I realized that while rigid plans are useful, maintaining flexibility is crucial to adapting to changing circumstances and new opportunities.
- Understanding the people impacted by changes became another focus, as their support and engagement are essential for successful implementation of whatever solution we are talking about.
- How could I help them explore the strategic options available while emphasizing the importance of not just looking at short-term gains but considering the bigger picture and the connections between various stakeholders.
- I also questioned the common assumption that leaders must have all the answers themselves. Embracing a collaborative mindset and valuing diverse perspectives can lead to richer, more effective solutions.

To achieve this, I expanded my perspective by adopting additional new mindsets. These shifts have revolutionized my approach. Building on the foundational **"Put Your Customer at the Center"** as the **#1 mindset**, I've uncovered seven additional mindsets that I describe below:

2. Be smarter with your resources: Efficient resource allocation is crucial for effective problem-solving. By optimizing resources, such as time, manpower, and finances, teams can maximize their impact and achieve better outcomes. This mindset encourages prioritization and strategic utilization of resources to address the most critical aspects of the problem.

3. Embrace adaptability over rigid plans: By prioritizing flexibility over predictability, teams can respond swiftly to changing circumstances. By recognizing that plans may need adjustment and being open to iteration. This approach encourages a mindset that values responsiveness and the ability to pivot based on evolving needs, fostering resilience and innovation.

4. Who's going to be impacted by the change? Considering the broader impact of proposed solutions is crucial for responsible decision-making. This mindset encourages stakeholders to assess how various groups, including employees, customers, and communities, will be affected by the proposed changes. By anticipating and addressing potential impacts, teams can mitigate risks and ensure smoother implementation.

5. See the bigger picture to understand connections. It involves zooming out from immediate issues to grasp how various elements within a system interact and influence one another. By recognizing these interconnections, one can appreciate the complexity of systems and anticipate how changes in one part may ripple throughout the entire system. This perspective enables a more comprehensive understanding of problems and solutions, helping teams avoid narrow, short-term fixes in favor of holistic, long-lasting approaches that account for systemic dynamics and future outcomes.

6. Acknowledge you don't know everything: Embracing humility and openness to learning is key to effective problem-solving. Recognizing that no individual or team has all the answers encourages curiosity, exploration, and collaboration. This mindset cultivates a culture of continuous improvement and innovation, where diverse perspectives are valued and leveraged.

7. Think critically about your choices. Strategic thinking guides decision-making by evaluating alternative courses of action and their potential outcomes. This mindset encourages teams to assess various strategic options and their implications, enabling informed decision-making aligned with organizational goals and objectives.

Lastly, embrace a Coaching Mindset:

8. How can you empower your staff, as opposed to just managing them? This would involve guidance, development, and support for employees, rather than just telling them what to do. It's about fostering a culture of continuous learning and improvement, where the manager empowers people so they can develop solutions, overcome challenges, and deliver results that move the needle.

Bottom line: Adopting these mindsets has empowered me to provide more structured and well-rounded advice. Each perspective enhances problem-solving with greater depth and creativity, leading to more effective and sustainable solutions. My invitation to others is to consider these mind shifts and apply them in their own environments. By experimenting with these new ways of thinking, you'll find that challenges are reframed and addressed more effectively. As the late Dr. Wayne Dyer[8] wisely noted, "Change the way you look at things and the things you look at will change."

The following examples showcase how adopting diverse mindsets can lead to successful problem-solving and innovation. By embracing different perspectives, you can unlock creative solutions and drive progress:

1. **Put your Customer at the Center:**

Worldwide: *Amazon* thrives on its customer-centric approach, continually innovating based on customer feedback, leading to features like one-click ordering and personalized recommendations (source: Brad Stone. The Everything Store, 2013) [9]

Alternatively, consider *Starbucks*, whose success is rooted in its customer-centric approach. The company constantly listens to customer feedback and adapts its offerings accordingly, such as introducing seasonal drinks and expanding its mobile ordering options, to enhance the overall customer experience. (Source: Knowledge at Wharton. Peter Fader, 2020) [10]

Canadian Public Sector: Immigration, Refugees and Citizenship Canada (IRCC) prioritizes customer satisfaction by streamlining application processes through online portals. By centering on user experience and feedback, IRCC adapts its services to meet the evolving needs of applicants, driving higher engagement and satisfaction. (Source: IRCC, 2022) [11]

2. Be Smarter with Your Resources:

Worldwide: Toyota's Just-in-Time (JIT) production system optimizes manufacturing by producing only what's needed when it's needed, reducing costs and enhancing productivity (source: Toyota) [12]

Another example could be *Walmart's* inventory management system, a prime illustration for optimizing resources. By implementing advanced algorithms and data analytics, Walmart minimizes stockouts and excess inventory, leading to improved efficiency and cost savings throughout its supply chain. (Source: inventoryy.com, 2023) [13]

Canadian Public Sector: The Canada Revenue Agency (CRA) adopted a digital-first approach for tax filings, leveraging digital technologies to streamline processes and reduce paperwork, ultimately improving user experience (source: CRA, 2023) [14]

3. Embrace adaptability over rigid plans:

Worldwide: *Apple's* iterative approach to software development allows for regular feedback and adjustments, speeding up time-to-market and improving product responsiveness (source: Owen Linzmeyer, 2004 & Leander Kahley, 2013) [15]

We might also consider *Nike*. They have embraced a strategy of iterative product launches. Rather than waiting to unveil an entire collection at once, Nike introduces new designs in scheduled releases throughout the year. This approach not only maintains a constant buzz around the brand but also enables Nike to gauge consumer preferences and trends more effectively. By iteratively refining its offerings based on real-time feedback and market insights, Nike stays ahead of the curve in delivering sought-after styles and experiences to its customers. (Source: Outsource Accelerator, 2021. Nike: Outsourcing Strategy) [16]

Canadian Public Sector: Public Services and Procurement Canada (PSPC) implements iterative updates to improve service delivery, enabling PSPC to adapt to emerging requirements and enhance the effectiveness of its operations (source: PSPC, 2023) [17]

4. Who's Going to be Impacted by the Change?

Worldwide: Coca-Cola's launch of Coca-Cola Zero Sugar reflects its commitment to consumer health concerns, aligning products with shifting preferences (source: Coca-Cola Company) [18]

We could also think of *Airbnb* when they expanded their services to include experiences and activities. At that point they engaged with local communities and stakeholders to understand their concerns and needs. By collaborating with hosts and local organizations, Airbnb ensures that its offerings align with the interests and preferences of both guests and hosts. (Source: Neil Patel, 2023) [19]

Canadian Public Sector: Health Canada's Health Products and Food Branch (HPFB) engages stakeholders in consultations to ensure diverse perspectives shape regulatory decisions, minimizing unintended consequences (source: Health Canada) [20]

5. Think Big Picture, Think Long Term:

Worldwide: Tesla's mission extends beyond electric vehicles, encompassing sustainable energy solutions like solar roofs, driving a holistic approach to environmental responsibility (source: Tesla) [21]

Another instance could be *Patagonia's* commitment to sustainability, which goes beyond just producing outdoor gear. They advocate for environmental conservation and social responsibility, engaging in initiatives like the "1% for the Planet" program and promoting fair labor practices. Patagonia's long-term vision aims to create a positive impact on the planet and society while maintaining profitability. (Source: Patagonia's Approach to Sustainability, 2023) [22]

Canadian Public Sector: Environment and Climate Change Canada (ECCC) formulates long-term climate action plans, emphasizing sustainable practices to address environmental challenges and foster resilience (source: ECCC) [23]

6. Acknowledge You Don't Know Everything:

Worldwide: Google encourages employees to devote time to side projects, leading to successful innovations like Gmail, fostering creativity and diverse input (source: Google) [24]

We might also look at Pixar Animation Studios, who foster innovation through a culture of experimentation and collaboration. Initiatives like "Braintrust" meetings, where directors and creative teams provide feedback on works in progress, highlight that great ideas can come from anyone within the organization. This approach has resulted in critically acclaimed films and breakthrough storytelling techniques. (Source: Ed Catmull, HBR Sep. 2008) [25]

Canadian Public Sector: The Canadian Space Agency (CSA) collaborates with academic institutions and private sector partners to foster innovation in space exploration and technology development. By embracing a collaborative approach and leveraging expertise from diverse stakeholders, CSA expands its knowledge base and advances cutting-edge research in space science and technology (Source: CSA) [26]

7. What Are My Strategic Choices?

Worldwide: *Netflix's* strategic pivot from DVD rentals to streaming positioned it as a market leader. Recognizing the evolving landscape and consumer preferences, Netflix capitalized on improving internet speeds to capitalize on the burgeoning streaming market (Netflix 2007) [27]

Moreover, another illustration could be Coca-Cola's strategic decision to diversify its product portfolio beyond carbonated beverages includes acquisitions of brands like Honest Tea and Smart Water. By recognizing changing consumer preferences towards healthier options, *Coca-Cola* strategically expanded its offerings to remain competitive in the beverage market. (Source: DataNext, Coca-Cola's Strategic Shift, 2023) [28]

Canadian Public Sector: The Treasury Board of Canada Secretariat (TBS) implements strategic procurement practices to optimize government spending and maximize value for taxpayers. By conducting thorough market analyses and adopting procurement strategies aligned with government priorities, TBS enhances transparency and accountability in government procurement processes (Source: TBS Procurement Strategy, 2023) [29]

8. How can I empower my staff vs Just manage them?

Worldwide: Microsoft has embraced a coaching mindset through its cultural transformation, focusing on a growth mindset as a foundational attribute. This framework emphasizes the importance of being a role model, staying curious, and genuinely caring about colleagues (Source: How Microsoft Uses a Growth Mindset to Develop Leaders, HBR 2016) [30]

Employee Engagement: By using interactive online modules, storytelling, and engaging tools like games and quizzes, Microsoft effectively promotes growth mindset behaviors among employees. This approach not only enhances engagement but also fosters a culture of continuous improvement. (Source: Growth Mindset and Coaching Culture at Microsoft) [31]

Continuous Learning: Microsoft rewards employees for their growth mindset and curiosity, which are crucial for driving business success. Platforms like Microsoft Viva Learning support employees in their learning journey by offering personalized recommendations and resources, ensuring they have the tools needed for ongoing development. (Source: How Microsoft Overhauled Its Approach to Growth Mindset) [32]

Canadian Public Sector: Here are a couple of examples that showcase how the Coaching Mindset approach is integrated into the professional development and leadership strategies within the Canadian Public Sector.

The Canada School of Public Service (CSPS) has developed a learning path that includes coaching as a fundamental part of developing and maximizing the potential of public service employees. This includes courses like "Introduction to Peer Coaching" and "Coaching for Effective Leadership," which apply the GROW Model to structure coaching conversations. The CSPS emphasizes that coaching is a reflective and co-creative process that offers individuals different ways of observing and interpreting situations, thereby tapping into their full potential. (Source: CSPS [n.d.] Coaching, Mentoring, and Networking Learning Path.) [33]

Another example is the concept of Generative Leadership in Canada's Public Sector. As highlighted by the Boston Consulting Group (BCG), It's a humanistic framework that fosters renewal and growth, especially during times of significant change. By leading with both the head and heart, this approach creates an environment where employees can excel, receive coaching, and be recognized for their contributions. Embracing Generative Leadership ensures a culture where individuals can perform at their best while being coached and recognized for it. (Source: Boston Consulting Group) [34]

Pillar 2. Best Practices from Proven Frameworks.

I trust that by now, I've piqued your interest in how these perspectives can transform your approach to challenges. By embracing these perspectives, you can unlock powerful benefits that go beyond theoretical concepts. Established frameworks and best practices are at your disposal, designed to enhance your problem-solving skills and drive superior results. Rather than starting from scratch, you can utilize these proven tools to your advantage.

If these ideas resonate with you, you'll be pleased to know that practical, tested methods are readily available. This section illustrates how these frameworks connect with the mindsets we've discussed and integrate seamlessly into my C.H.A.N.G.E.© framework, ensuring a cohesive approach to your challenges.

Reflecting on my journey, I realize that if I had known these mindsets and frameworks 20 years ago, I could have achieved significant success much sooner. And although I didn't have a coach to turn to then, I'm here to provide you with the guidance and support you need now.

1. Design Thinking:

> It relates with the **"Put your customer at the center"** mindset.
>
> **What it is.** Design Thinking puts your customer front and center. By deeply understanding their needs, you'll spark innovation, foster collaboration, and create solutions they truly love.
>
> **Why Design Thinking matters.**
>
> - **User-Centered Solutions:** Design Thinking underlines empathizing with end-users, ensuring solutions are tailored to their needs and pain points. This leads to higher satisfaction and engagement.
> - **Innovation and Creativity:** It fosters a culture of innovation by challenging assumptions and encouraging unconventional ideas. This mindset leads to breakthrough solutions for complex challenges.

- **Iterative Problem-Solving:** The iterative approach allows for rapid prototyping and user feedback, reducing the risk of failure and enabling early course corrections.
- **Cross-Functional Collaboration:** Design Thinking brings together diverse perspectives, facilitating richer insights and more comprehensive solutions through collaborative problem-solving.

How Design Thinking Works:

- **Empathize:** Deeply understand your users. Uncover their needs, challenges, and desires through observation and conversation.
- **Define:** Clearly articulate the problem. Transform user insights into a focused challenge statement.
- **Ideate:** Unleash your creativity. Generate a wealth of innovative solutions through brainstorming and idea generation.
- **Prototype:** Bring ideas to life. Quickly create tangible representations of your concepts to test and refine.
- **Test:** Learn from your users. Gather feedback on your prototypes to iterate and improve.

By following this human-centered process, you'll create solutions that truly resonate with your audience and ultimately achieve better outcomes. I'm sure it will become clearer if we look below at Exhibit #5, which represents the so-called Design Thinking Double Diamond process, which guides the journey from problems to solutions through four phases:

1. **Diverge – Discover:** Explore and understand the problem space to uncover a wide range of insights and opportunities.
2. **Converge – Define:** Narrow down insights to define clear problem statements and focus on specific challenges.
3. **Diverge – Develop:** Generate diverse ideas and solutions through brainstorming and prototyping.
4. **Converge – Deliver:** Refine and select the most promising solutions, ensuring they are **desirable by the client, technically feasible** and **financially viable** before implementation.

Exhibit #5

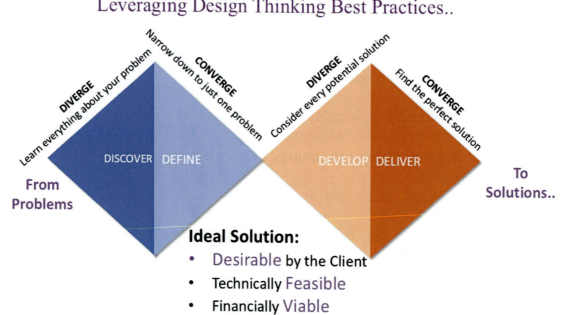

*Altered version of the original Double Diamond model by the British Design Council

In other words, the Design Thinking Double Diamond is a structured process that helps teams solve problems effectively. It's split into two phases: the first focuses on exploring and defining the core issue, while the second is about brainstorming and refining solutions. This method ensures that teams first understand the real problem before jumping into solutions.

The ultimate goal is to create solutions that are desirable by the client (meeting actual needs), technically feasible (can be built and implemented), and financially viable (make economic sense). This ensures that the solution is not only innovative but also practical and sustainable.

Furthermore, as shown in Exhibit #6, the six change steps of the C.H.A.N.G.E. Model© align seamlessly with the Double Diamond process, from Clarify Goals to Generate Solutions and Evaluate Progress. This alignment illustrates how two sequential, repeatable processes are in synch, allowing us to continue leveraging the structured, iterative nature of the C.H.A.N.G.E. Model© to drive continuous improvement and adaptation effectively.

Exhibit #6

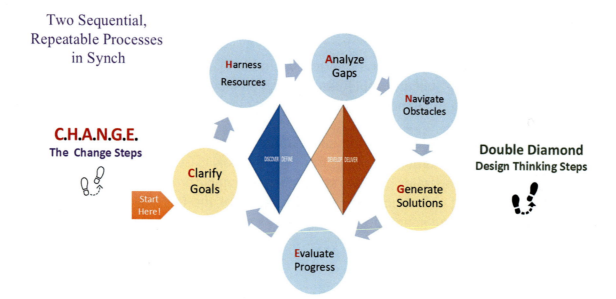

Here are 7 simple steps to effectively apply Design Thinking with your team:

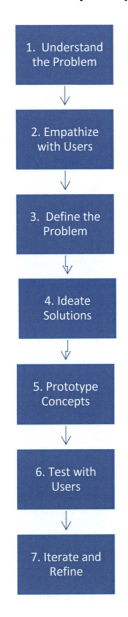

1. Clearly identify the challenge your team aims to solve, focusing on understanding it from the end-user's perspective to ensure you address their needs and pain points.

2. Gain insights into users' needs, motivations, and behaviors through interviews, observations, and surveys. This research helps tailor your solution to fit user preferences and enhance their experience.

3. Based on your research, clearly define the problem statement or opportunity, outlining the project's goals, objectives, and any constraints.

4. Encourage creative thinking and explore diverse solutions through brainstorming and techniques like mind mapping, aiming to uncover innovative approaches to the problem.

5. Create simple, low-fidelity prototypes or mock-ups of the most promising ideas. These prototypes allow you to quickly visualize and test different concepts.

6. Test the prototypes with users to gather feedback on their interactions and experiences. Use this feedback to validate assumptions, identify issues, and refine your solution.

7. Continuously improve the prototypes based on user feedback. Iterate through the design and testing phases until the solution effectively meets user needs and performs well.

Improving processes in Canadian public service organizations, particularly with Design Thinking, involves several key challenges:

Technological Complexity: As highlighted in the Canada Border Services Agency's "Strategic Plan 2021-2025," integrating new technologies to enhance border operations can be difficult. Understanding and implementing these technologies, especially through user-centric approaches like Design Thinking, requires overcoming significant complexity.

User Perspective Integration: The Office of the Auditor General's "2020 Fall Reports" reveal that government programs often miss the mark due to insufficient user perspective. Effective Design Thinking must address these gaps by incorporating comprehensive stakeholder input to avoid such pitfalls.

Interdisciplinary Collaboration: The Department of National Defense's "Defense Plan 2022-2023" stresses the need for cross-departmental collaboration. Achieving this collaboration, especially when applying Design Thinking, can be challenging due to siloed operations and differing departmental priorities.

Middle Management Resistance: The Royal Canadian Mounted Police's "Strategic Priority Plan 2021-2025" points out a commitment to innovation. However, conflicting values and resistance to change among middle managers can hinder the adoption of Design Thinking principles, impacting progress and user-centric improvements.

Addressing these challenges requires not only strong leadership and effective communication but also a concerted effort to foster a culture of innovation, collaboration, and continuous improvement. By embracing Design Thinking principles like empathy and user-centricity, public service organizations can overcome these obstacles and drive meaningful improvements in service delivery and operational efficiency.

Consulting Case Study #2:

In a recent engagement with a public sector organization, our client faced the challenge of modernizing service delivery within a key sector. While I cannot share specific details of the project due to confidentiality, the goal was to improve the effectiveness of modernization efforts by integrating human-centered design principles. The approach helped their teams identify gaps and opportunities, driving digital and service transformation to enhance overall service delivery.

As a consultant, I led the strategic planning and development of the Service Design discipline for the Justice Sector using a Design Thinking approach. I began by clearly identifying the challenge from the end-user's perspective, ensuring our solutions addressed their needs and pain points. Through in-depth research involving field studies, interviews, diary studies, and usability testing, I gained valuable insights into user needs, motivations, and behaviors. This information informed the problem statement and project goals, guiding our design process.

I encouraged creative thinking through brainstorming and mind mapping, exploring diverse solutions and creating simple, low-fidelity prototypes of the most promising ideas. These prototypes were tested with users to gather feedback, validate assumptions, and refine our solutions. This iterative process allowed us to continuously improve the prototypes based on user input, ensuring that the final solutions effectively met user needs and performed well.

The project resulted in a robust service design framework successfully applied to various modernization projects within the Justice Sector. This framework enabled the ministries to gain a deeper understanding of user needs, address service delivery gaps, and enhance overall program effectiveness. By integrating service design principles and employing Design Thinking methodology, the project led to more efficient, user-centered digital and service transformations, ultimately improving service delivery across the Justice Sector.

Related Literature on Design Thinking:

- "Design Thinking: Understanding How Designers Think and Work" by Nigel Cross - This book introduces the principles and practices of Design Thinking, exploring the mindset and methods used by designers to solve complex problems creatively.
- "Change by Design: How Design Thinking Transforms Organizations and Inspires Innovation" by Tim Brown - Tim Brown, CEO of IDEO, offers insights into how Design Thinking can drive innovation and organizational change. The book provides real-world examples and case studies of how Design Thinking has been applied successfully in various contexts.
- "Sprint: How to Solve Big Problems and Test New Ideas in Just Five Days" by Jake Knapp, John Zeratsky, and Braden Kowitz - This book introduces the concept of the design sprint,

a five-day process for rapidly prototyping and testing ideas. It offers practical guidance and tools for applying Design Thinking principles to accelerate innovation.
- "The Design of Everyday Things" by Don Norman - While not solely focused on Design Thinking, this classic book explores the principles of user-centered design and usability. It offers valuable insights into how design influences user behavior and perception, providing a foundational understanding for applying Design Thinking principles.
- "Creative Confidence: Unleashing the Creative Potential Within Us All" by Tom Kelley and David Kelley - This book explores how to cultivate creativity and innovation within individuals and organizations. It offers practical strategies and exercises for developing creative confidence and applying Design Thinking principles to solve complex problems.

These resources provide a comprehensive foundation for understanding and applying Design Thinking principles to your team's projects and initiatives.

2. Lean Principles:

They connect with the mindset "**Be smarter with your resources**".

What it is. Lean is a proven approach to dramatically improve efficiency, reduce waste, and boost productivity. Born from Toyota's manufacturing system, Lean focuses on creating more value with less work.

Why Lean matters.

- **Slash waste:** Identify and eliminate non-value-adding activities, saving time, money, and resources.
- **Accelerate processes:** Streamline workflows, reduce bottlenecks, and deliver products or services faster.
- **Optimize resource use:** Produce only what's needed, when it's needed, preventing overproduction and inventory buildup.
- **Foster continuous improvement:** Cultivate a culture of innovation where teams constantly seek better ways to work.
- **Maximize output:** Focus on activities that truly add value, ensuring your team is working smarter, not harder.

How it works.

Lean **systematically identifies and eliminates** waste through tools like value stream mapping and Kaizen (continuous improvement). By analyzing workflows and standardizing processes, Lean **creates smoother operations** and **a more engaged workforce**.

In essence, **Lean is about achieving more with less. It's a balance of doing the right things (effectiveness) and doing things right (efficiency).** By adopting Lean principles, you can significantly enhance your organization's performance and bottom line.

I'm sure it will become clearer if we look at Exhibit #7 below.

Once again, keeping in mind the C.H.A.N.G.E.© Process reviewed previously, we can see a clear alignment between it and the Lean Cycle. Both frameworks utilize a systematic approach to driving improvement and efficiency. For instance, the Lean Cycle's steps—ranging from "Identify Value" to "Empower Team Members"—parallel the stages of the C.H.A.N.G.E.© Process, from "Clarify Goals" to "Generate Solutions."

By starting with "Identify Value," we set the foundation for clarifying our goals, which ultimately leads to empowering our team to independently generate effective solutions. This approach ensures that our initial focus on value directly supports our goal of fostering team autonomy and innovation.

Essentially, we could say that **the Lean Cycle itself represents a change management challenge**, and at the same time, that **the C.H.A.N.G.E.© Process is a Lean Process in itself.** This integrated approach ensures that both improvement and change management efforts are cohesive and impactful.

Exhibit #7

So how can I use it?

Here's a simplified 7 steps guide to applying Lean Principles to your team:

1. **Boost efficiency and reduce costs** by teaching your team Lean principles to maximize value and minimize process waste.

2. **Enhance customer satisfaction** by clearly defining and delivering what customers truly value.

3. **Streamline operations** by mapping your value delivery process, pinpointing waste, and eliminating unnecessary steps.

4. **Accelerate delivery and improve quality** by targeting and eliminating waste, such as overproduction, wait times, and defects.

5. **Cultivate a culture of innovation** by empowering your team to identify and implement continuous improvements.

6. **Strengthen employee engagement** by giving your team ownership over process improvements and providing necessary support.

7. **Drive sustainable growth** by consistently monitoring Lean initiatives, gathering feedback, and adapting for ongoing success.

What are some challenges that could be encountered during start-up?

Improving processes in Canadian public service organizations faces significant challenges, as evidenced by various reports and documents that I assembled during my research. For instance, within the Canada Revenue Agency (CRA), the document "Annual Report to Parliament 2021-2022" highlights the complexities of tax-related processes and the importance of efficient procedures to ensure accurate tax collection and refund disbursement (CRA, 2022). It's within this context that the lack of proper training in Lean methodologies becomes particularly problematic, potentially leading to inefficiencies and errors in tax administration.

Similarly, at Health Canada, the "Departmental Results Report 2020-2021" underscores the importance of effective management practices to ensure the safety and well-being of Canadians (Health Canada, 2021). However, resistance to change from management and employees can hinder the adoption of Lean approaches, impeding efforts to improve processes and enhance service delivery within the department.

In the case of Service Canada, responsible for delivering a wide range of citizen services, the "Departmental Plan 2022-2023" emphasizes the need for efficient and client-focused service delivery (Service Canada, 2023). Insufficient allocation of financial resources may hamper Service Canada's ability to invest in Lean training and infrastructure, limiting its capacity to streamline processes and enhance service quality for Canadians.

Furthermore, within the Department of Indigenous Services Canada, the "2021-2022 Departmental Plan" highlights the importance of building strong relationships with Indigenous peoples and supporting self-determination and self-government (Indigenous Services Canada, 2022). However, cultural barriers and hierarchical structures within the organization may impede efforts to implement Lean principles effectively, hindering progress toward these goals.

Lastly, the importance of clear key performance indicators (KPIs) in monitoring progress and ensuring alignment with organizational objectives is underscored in documents such as the "Departmental Plan 2021-2022" of Public Services and Procurement Canada (Public Services and Procurement Canada, 2020). Without robust KPIs, public service organizations may struggle to track the effectiveness of Lean initiatives and make data-driven decisions to drive continuous improvement.

Related Literature on Lean Principles.

Extensive research supports Lean's transformative power. Studies consistently demonstrate its ability to drastically reduce costs, enhance efficiency, and improve customer satisfaction. By drawing on this knowledge base, you can accelerate your Lean journey and achieve remarkable results. Here I propose some readings that I hope you find interesting:

- "Lean Thinking: Banish Waste and Create Wealth in Your Corporation" by James P. Womack and Daniel T. Jones - This seminal book introduces the core concepts of Lean Thinking and provides practical guidance on how to apply Lean Principles in various organizational contexts.
- "The Toyota Way: 14 Management Principles from the World's Greatest Manufacturer" by Jeffrey K. Liker - This book explores the principles and practices that have made Toyota a leader in lean manufacturing. It offers valuable insights into how to apply Lean Principles to improve operational efficiency and quality.
- "Lean Six Sigma for Dummies" by John Morgan and Martin Brenig-Jones - This accessible guide introduces Lean Six Sigma, a methodology that combines Lean Principles with Six Sigma techniques for process improvement. It offers practical tips and case studies for implementing Lean Six Sigma in organizations of all sizes.
- "Lean Startup: How Today's Entrepreneurs Use Continuous Innovation to Create Radically Successful Businesses" by Eric Ries - While not solely focused on Lean Principles in a traditional manufacturing context, this book explores how Lean Thinking can be applied to startups and entrepreneurial ventures to achieve rapid growth and innovation.
- "Gemba Kaizen: A Commonsense Approach to a Continuous Improvement Strategy" by Masaaki Imai - This book delves into the concept of Gemba Kaizen, which emphasizes making small, incremental improvements at the workplace (Gemba) to achieve significant results over time. It offers practical advice and case studies for implementing Kaizen principles in organizations.
- "Lean Solutions: How Companies and Customers Can Create Value and Wealth Together" by James P. Womack and Daniel T. Jones

3. Agile Practices:

   Is in line with **"Embrace adaptability over rigid plans"** mindset.

   What it is. Agile practices promote iterative development, collaboration, and adaptability. By breaking down projects into smaller, manageable tasks and embracing change, teams can respond more effectively to evolving requirements and deliver high-quality solutions efficiently.

   Why Agile Practices Matter:

   - **Flexibility and Adaptability:** Agile Practices enable teams to respond quickly and effectively to changing requirements, market conditions, and customer feedback. This flexibility allows organizations to adapt their strategies and priorities in real-time, leading to faster delivery of valuable solutions.
   - **Improved Collaboration:** Agile practices foster close collaboration and open communication among team members, stakeholders, and customers. This transparency and shared responsibility harness collective expertise and insights, driving innovation and effective problem-solving.
   - **Increased Productivity:** Agile practices facilitate a steady work pace by breaking projects into manageable tasks (iterations or sprints). This approach minimizes delays and bottlenecks, enhancing productivity and efficiency through continuous incremental value delivery.
   - **Enhanced Quality:** Agile practices focus on frequent delivery of working solutions, which allows for early and regular feedback. This continuous loop helps identify and address issues quickly, leading to higher-quality deliverables that better meet user needs and expectations.
   - **Customer Satisfaction:** Agile practices prioritize delivering timely value to customers. Involving customers throughout the development process and providing incremental improvements ensures that the final product aligns closely with their requirements and preferences, resulting in greater satisfaction and loyalty.

How Agile Practices Work:

- **Iterative Development:** Agile practices break projects into smaller iterations or sprints, usually lasting 1-4 weeks. Each iteration delivers a subset of features, enabling teams to incrementally build and refine the product. This approach ensures continuous progress and adaptability.
- **Cross-Functional Teams:** Agile practices promote cross-functional teams with diverse skills and expertise. These self-organizing teams make collaborative decisions, incorporating multiple perspectives and enhancing the development process through collective input.
- **Continuous Planning and Adaptation:** Agile practices emphasize ongoing planning and adaptation based on feedback and evolving requirements. Teams regularly review progress, adjust plans, and reprioritize tasks, ensuring they consistently deliver maximum value to customers.
- **Daily Stand-up Meetings:** Agile practices include daily stand-up meetings (or "daily scrums"), where team members update progress, address obstacles, and coordinate daily activities. These brief, focused meetings maintain team alignment and visibility into progress.
- **Regular Reviews and Retrospectives:** Agile practices feature regular reviews and retrospectives at the end of each iteration or sprint. Reviews showcase completed work to stakeholders for feedback, while retrospectives allow teams to reflect on their processes and identify improvement areas.

By understanding why Agile Practices matter and how they work, public organizations can leverage this framework to drive innovation, improve collaboration, and deliver value to customers more efficiently and effectively.

For clarity, let's examine Exhibit #8 to explain Agile and its connection to the C.H.A.N.G.E.© Process. Agile mirrors our process by starting with high-level planning, progressing through Sprints to address obstacles, and concluding with a Sprint retrospective to evaluate progress. This iterative cycle of planning, executing, and reviewing makes the Sprint cycle a change management challenge in and on itself, as it demands continuous adaptation to new insights and feedback.

To further illustrate, please refer to Exhibit #9. In Agile, the process starts with the Product Vision, defining goals and strategic alignment, and is supported by the Product Roadmap, which outlines features to achieve that vision. Each Sprint delivers incremental improvements, demanding frequent adjustments and effective change management to ensure positive outcomes and team productivity.

Exhibit #8

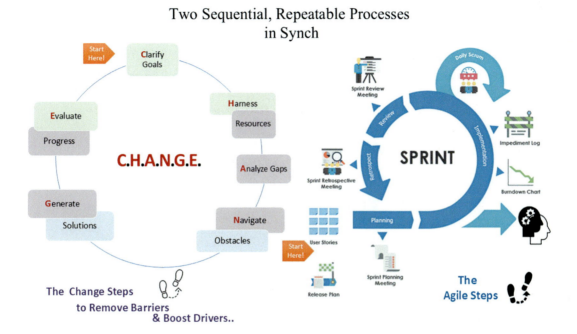

Exhibit #9

A Roadmap to Business Value

Start Here!

Stage 1: Product Vision
Description: The goals for the product and its alignment with the organization's strategy
Owner: Product Owner
Frequency: At least annually

Stage 2: Product Roadmap
Description: Holistic view of product features that fulfill the Product Vision
Owner: Product Owner
Frequency: At least biannually

Stage 3: Release Planning
Description: Timely releases of specific product functionalities
Owner: Product Owner
Frequency: At least quarterly

Stage 4: Sprint Planning
Description: Establish specific goals & tasks for each iteration
Owner: Product Owner & Development team
Frequency: At start of each sprint

Stage 5: Daily Scrum
Description: Establish / coordinate daily priorities
Owner: Dev team
Frequency: Daily

24 Hours

Stage 6: Sprint Review
Description: Demonstrate working product
Owner: Product Owner & Dev team
Frequency: At end of each sprint

Stage 7: Team Retrospective
Description: Team refinement of environment & processes to optimize efficiency
Owner: Scrum team
Frequency: At the end of each sprint

Sprint Cycle 1 to 4 weeks

From Preparation → **To Execution**

48

My bottom-line is that to effectively manage the Agile Sprint cycle, we must integrate change management practices to navigate continuous adaptations. Use Product Vision and Roadmap to guide each Sprint, ensuring alignment with goals and strategic objectives. Regularly review progress and adjust plans to maintain productivity and drive successful outcomes.

Integrating Agile with Traditional Project Management for Optimal Efficiency.

Now, what about project management? We haven't said anything about it yet, and although this is normally outsourced to professional project managers, it is worth going over some concepts now that we are on the subject. So, let's touch on it briefly.

While Agile is effective in dynamic environments, a solid structure is also essential for guiding project execution. Combining Agile with traditional project management principles offers a balanced approach, providing both flexibility and structure. In most government projects, a blend of Agile and Waterfall is common. Therefore, I recommend using a hybrid scheme that integrates both methodologies, ensuring better outcomes.

The framework I propose—Envision, Speculate, Explore, Adapt, Close—mirrors Project Management Institute's PMBOK® Guide[35] (Project Management Body of Knowledge) phases (Initiate, Plan, Execute, Monitor & Control, Close) with an iterative focus, ensuring effective execution and success in various project environments. To illustrate these concepts, please look at the following visual:

Exhibit #10

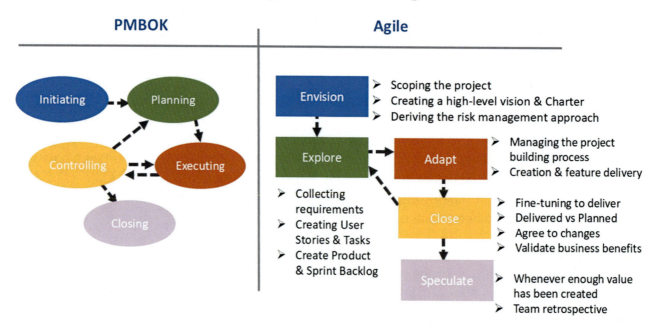

1. **Envision** parallels the **Initiating** phase by setting the project's vision, scope, and charter, and establishing a risk management approach.
2. **Speculate** aligns with **Planning** by gathering requirements, creating user stories and tasks, and building the product and sprint backlog.
3. **Explore** corresponds to **Executing** through managing the project building process and delivering features.
4. **Adapt** mirrors **Controlling & Monitoring** by fine-tuning delivery, comparing delivered outcomes with planned objectives, agreeing to changes, and validating benefits.
5. **Close** reflects the **Closing** phase by determining when sufficient value has been created and conducting a team retrospective.

By integrating both Agile and traditional project management approaches, you create a robust framework that provides clear direction and effective risk management while maintaining Agile's flexibility and adaptability. This hybrid method balances stability with agility, leading to more efficient project management and improved outcomes. It ensures a solid foundation for your projects, allows for incremental value delivery, and enhances overall project efficiency and effectiveness.

7 Easy Steps to Apply Agile Practices:

1. Equip your team with Agile knowledge, understanding the core principles and values.

2. Select an Agile framework that aligns with your needs: (*Scrum*: Emphasizes iterative development and cross-functional teams. *Kanban*: Focuses on visualizing workflow. *Extreme Programming (XP)*: Prioritizes test-driven development).

3. Define clear objectives for your Agile journey, ensuring alignment with organizational vision.

4. Create cross-functional, self-organizing teams to foster ownership and innovation.

5. Implement core Agile rituals like daily stand-ups, sprint planning, and retrospectives.

6. Foster a culture of learning and adaptation through regular reflection.

7. Prioritize feedback from stakeholders and customers to refine your Agile approach.

What are some challenges that could be encountered during start-up?

Improving processes within Canadian public service organizations, particularly through the adoption of Agile Practices, confronts various challenges that necessitate careful consideration and strategic planning. For instance, within Employment and Social Development Canada (ESDC), responsible for managing complex social programs and services, the "Departmental Plan 2021-2022" highlights the importance of innovation and agility in responding to evolving needs (ESDC, 2021). However, resistance to change among employees accustomed to traditional project management approaches can hinder the successful implementation of Agile methodologies. Overcoming this resistance requires not only effective change management strategies but also efforts to foster a culture of experimentation and continuous improvement within the organization.

Similarly, in the Department of Fisheries and Oceans Canada (DFO), tasked with conserving and managing Canada's aquatic resources, the "Report on Plans and Priorities 2022-2023" underscores the need for adaptable and responsive approaches to address complex environmental challenges (DFO, 2022). However, incorrect planning poses a significant risk to the success of Agile initiatives within the department. Inadequate understanding of Agile principles and practices may lead to misaligned objectives, unrealistic timelines, and insufficient allocation of resources, ultimately undermining the effectiveness of improvement efforts. To mitigate these risks, DFO must invest in comprehensive training and guidance in Agile methodologies, coupled with robust project planning processes to ensure alignment with organizational goals and objectives.

Moreover, in the Canada Revenue Agency (CRA), responsible for administering tax laws and programs, the "Departmental Plan 2021-2022" emphasizes the importance of modernizing service delivery and improving client experiences (CRA, 2021). However, insufficient resources and a lack of buy-in from key stakeholders can hinder Agile implementation efforts. Without adequate support from senior leadership and sufficient resources allocated to Agile teams, projects may struggle to progress effectively, leading to delays and suboptimal outcomes. Addressing these challenges requires a concerted effort to engage stakeholders, build organizational capacity in Agile methodologies, and foster a culture of collaboration and innovation across the agency.

Related Literature on Agile Practices:

- "Scrum: The Art of Doing Twice the Work in Half the Time" by Jeff Sutherland - This book introduces Scrum, one of the most widely used Agile frameworks. Jeff Sutherland, one of the co-creators of Scrum, shares insights and practical tips for implementing Scrum practices to improve productivity and efficiency.
- "Kanban: Successful Evolutionary Change for Your Technology Business" by David J. Anderson - This book introduces the Kanban method, a flexible Agile framework for managing work. David J. Anderson explores how Kanban principles can be applied to visualize work, limit work in progress, and optimize workflow to improve delivery and quality.
- "Agile Estimating and Planning" by Mike Cohn - This book offers practical guidance on Agile project estimation and planning techniques. Mike Cohn explores how to use Agile practices such as user stories, relative sizing, and velocity tracking to estimate and plan projects accurately and adaptively.
- "Lean Agile Software Development: Achieving Enterprise Agility" by Alan Shalloway, Guy Beaver, and James R. Trott - This book explores how Lean principles can be combined with Agile practices to achieve enterprise agility. It offers insights into scaling Agile practices across large organizations and overcoming common challenges in Agile adoption.

These resources provide valuable insights and practical guidance for implementing Agile Practices effectively within your team or organization.

4. Change Management:

Is consistent with the question **"Who's going to be impacted by the Change?"**

What it is. Change management frameworks help organizations navigate transitions effectively. By proactively addressing resistance to change, communicating effectively, and providing support to stakeholders, teams can facilitate smooth implementation of solutions.

Why Change Management Matters:

- **Facilitating Organizational Adaptability:** Change is inevitable in today's dynamic business environment. Change Management frameworks help organizations adapt to

new technologies, market conditions, and strategic initiatives more effectively, enabling them to stay competitive and resilient in the face of uncertainty.
- **Minimizing Disruption:** Change can disrupt workflows, processes, and routines within an organization. Change Management frameworks help minimize disruption by providing a structured approach to planning, communicating, and implementing change. This reduces the negative impact on productivity, morale, and performance.
- **Managing Resistance:** Change often triggers resistance from stakeholders who may feel uncertain or uncomfortable with the proposed changes. Change Management frameworks help identify and address sources of resistance, fostering buy-in and engagement among stakeholders to ensure successful change adoption.
- **Enhancing Employee Engagement:** Effective Change Management promotes transparency, involvement, and collaboration among employees throughout the change process. By involving employees in decision-making, soliciting their input, and providing opportunities for feedback, organizations can foster a sense of ownership and commitment to change initiatives.
- **Driving Business Results:** Ultimately, Change Management is about driving positive business outcomes. Whether it's improving operational efficiency, launching new products or services, or transforming organizational culture, Change Management frameworks help organizations realize the intended benefits of change initiatives more quickly and effectively.

How Change Management Works. Introducing a Proven Change Management Cycle:

To ensure successful change initiatives, it's essential to follow a structured approach. The Change Management Cycle outlined below is based on established best practices from leading frameworks such as John Kotter's 8-Step Change Model[36] and Prosci's ADKAR Model[37]. This approach integrates key principles that have been validated through extensive application and research in the field of change management.

1. **Assessing Readiness for Change**: Begin by evaluating your organization's readiness for change. This includes understanding the organizational culture, leadership support, and capacity for change. This step sets the foundation for effective change management.

2. **Defining the Change Vision and Objectives**: Establish a clear vision and objectives for the change. Define what the change will involve, why it's necessary, and what outcomes are desired. Clear and consistent communication of the vision is crucial for aligning stakeholders.
3. **Engaging Stakeholders**: Identify and engage key stakeholders. Understand their concerns and perspectives and involve them in the change process. Effective communication and relationship-building are vital for gaining support and ensuring a smooth transition.
4. **Developing a Change Management Plan**: Create a detailed plan that outlines strategies, risks, roles, responsibilities, and communication channels. This plan should also include mechanisms for stakeholder support and address potential challenges.
5. **Implementing the Change**: Execute the change initiative systematically, including training, process updates, and resource allocation. Regular monitoring and feedback will help track progress and address issues promptly.

By leveraging this structured approach, you can significantly improve your change management efforts and achieve successful outcomes. The C.H.A.N.G.E.© Process builds on this foundation, offering a tailored framework that enhances goal setting, resource management, and obstacle navigation. Let's explore how this process integrates these elements with the following visual:

Exhibit #11

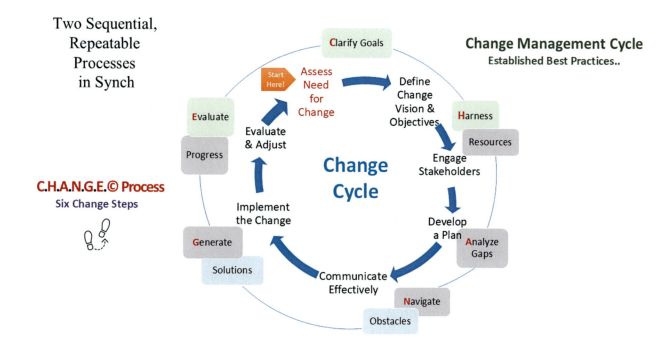

The C.H.A.N.G.E.© Process offers a comprehensive framework that aligns closely with the traditional Change Management Cycle but provides a more integrated and dynamic approach:

1. **Clarify Goals (Assessment & Vision)**: Directly ties to assessing readiness for change and defining the change vision. This step ensures that goals are clearly articulated and aligned with the organization's capacity and objectives.
2. **Harness Resources (Planning)**: Corresponds to developing a change management plan. It focuses on identifying and allocating resources effectively to support the change initiative, addressing potential risks, and setting up support mechanisms.
3. **Analyze Gaps (Engagement)**: Complements stakeholder engagement by identifying gaps between current states and desired outcomes. This step involves understanding stakeholder needs and ensuring that the change addresses these gaps.
4. **Navigate Obstacles (Implementation)**: Aligns with implementing the change. This step involves managing challenges and barriers during the change process, ensuring smooth execution, and adapting as necessary.
5. **Generate Solutions (Implementation & Adaptation)**: Mirrors aspects of implementation and adaptation, focusing on refining solutions, addressing issues, and adjusting based on feedback and progress.
6. **Evaluate Progress (Monitoring & Closing)**: Directly parallels monitoring progress and evaluating outcomes. This step ensures that the change is achieving the desired results and allows for adjustments to enhance effectiveness.

Based on my practical experience and the insights gained from applying the C.H.A.N.G.E.© Process in real-world scenarios, I consider it the best option due to its holistic and flexible approach, which covers all crucial aspects of change management from goal clarification to progress evaluation. It emphasizes continuous adaptation and feedback, ensuring responsiveness to real-time challenges and evolving needs. By optimizing resource use, addressing gaps, and proactively navigating obstacles, it ensures a seamless transition and effective implementation. Regular progress evaluation allows for ongoing improvements, making the C.H.A.N.G.E.© Process a dynamic, integrated approach that aligns with organizational goals and enhances overall change management success.

I invite you to put it to the test.

7 Easy Steps to Apply Change Management:

How can I apply it on my team? Applying the Change Management Cycle in your team involves practical steps to align design thinking with strategic goals. Let's explore how you can do this:

1. Assess the specific changes required within your team or organization, understanding the underlying reasons, challenges, and opportunities.

2. Define and communicate a clear, compelling vision for the change, detailing its benefits and alignment with organizational goals and values.

3. Identify and involve stakeholders from the beginning. Gather their input, address their concerns, and ensure they understand and support the change vision.

4. Create a detailed plan that includes strategies, tactics, resources, roles, responsibilities, and metrics for tracking progress and success.

5. Maintain transparent, consistent, and empathetic communication throughout the process. Keep stakeholders informed about the change's rationale and impact, addressing concerns and providing support.

6. Execute the change in a structured manner, providing necessary training and resources. Monitor the implementation closely to address any issues or obstacles.

7. Continuously evaluate progress and gather feedback. Adjust strategies and tactics as needed to address any challenges and ensure the change is successful.

What are some challenges that could be encountered during start-up?

Improving processes within Canadian public service organizations, especially when introducing new methodologies, faces a multitude of challenges that must be addressed to ensure successful implementation. One significant obstacle is resistance to change among employees, as highlighted in reports such as the "Change Management Best Practices Guide" published by the Treasury Board of Canada Secretariat (TBS, n.d.). This comprehensive guide outlines strategies for managing resistance to change and emphasizes the importance of addressing employees' concerns and providing support throughout the transition process. For instance, within the Canada Border Services Agency (CBSA), responsible for border security and immigration enforcement, resistance to change may arise from frontline officers accustomed to traditional procedures. Strategies such as targeted training programs, change champions networks, and transparent communication can help mitigate resistance and foster a culture of openness to change (CBSA, 2021).

Additionally, inadequate leadership support can impede progress and undermine change initiatives within public service organizations. Effective leadership is crucial in championing change, setting clear objectives, and providing direction. However, as noted in the "Public Service Employee Survey" conducted by the Office of the Chief Human Resources Officer (OCHRO, n.d.), some employees may perceive a lack of leadership support for change initiatives. This lack of support can erode trust and confidence in the change process, making it challenging to garner buy-in and commitment from employees. To address this challenge, leaders must actively engage with employees, communicate the rationale behind the changes, and demonstrate their commitment to supporting employees through the transition.

Moreover, a lack of clear objectives and communication can exacerbate resistance to change and impede progress towards process improvement. Without transparent communication channels and well-defined goals, employees may feel uncertain about the purpose and expected outcomes of the changes. In the Department of Finance Canada, responsible for developing fiscal and economic policies, the "Departmental Plan 2021-2022" emphasizes the importance of clear communication and goal setting to drive organizational effectiveness (Finance Canada, 2021). By establishing clear objectives and fostering open communication channels, public service organizations can help alleviate uncertainty and enhance employee engagement, thereby facilitating successful change management processes.

Related Literature on Change Management:

- "Leading Change" by John P. Kotter - This classic book by renowned change management expert John Kotter outlines an eight-step process for leading successful organizational change. It offers practical insights and real-world examples to help leaders navigate complex change initiatives effectively.
- "Change Management: The People Side of Change" by Jeffrey M. Hiatt and Timothy J. Creasey - This book provides a practical guide to change management, focusing on the human aspects of change. It offers tools, templates, and case studies to help leaders and change agents implement effective change management strategies.
- "Change Management: Principles and Practice" by Rory Burke - This comprehensive textbook offers an overview of change management principles, theories, and practices. It covers topics such as change models, resistance to change, and communication strategies, providing a solid foundation for implementing change effectively.
- "The Heart of Change: Real-Life Stories of How People Change Their Organizations" by John P. Kotter and Dan S. Cohen - This book explores the importance of emotions and storytelling in driving successful change. It presents real-life case studies and practical insights into how leaders can inspire and motivate people to embrace change.
- These resources provide valuable insights and practical guidance for applying change management principles and practices to your team or organization.

5. Systems Thinking:

Is linked to "See the bigger picture to understand connections" mindset.

What it is. System thinking fosters a comprehensive view of interconnected components and their relationships within a system. By embracing this approach, teams can uncover key leverage points and create solutions that target root causes rather than just addressing symptoms. This approach enhances problem-solving effectiveness and promotes sustainable improvements.

Why Systems Thinking Matters:

- **Broader Perspective:** Adopting a Systems Thinking Mindset helps leaders and employees to move beyond their immediate roles and consider the wider impact of their actions. This approach enhances awareness of the broader organizational system, ensuring all components work together harmoniously for greater success.
- **Understanding Complexity:** In today's interconnected and rapidly changing world, organizations face increasingly complex challenges that cannot be addressed by isolated solutions. Systems Thinking provides a framework for understanding the interconnectedness of various components within a system, helping organizations navigate complexity more effectively.
- **Leveraging Opportunities:** Systems Thinking allows teams to identify key leverage points where minor changes can lead to major improvements. By understanding system structures and feedback loops, organizations can focus interventions where they will be most impactful.
- **Avoiding Unintended Effects:** Unlike traditional methods that often address symptoms, Systems Thinking reveals root causes and anticipates potential side effects. This leads to more sustainable, resilient solutions and minimizes the risk of unintended consequences.
- **Fostering Innovation:** By examining interconnected relationships and challenging existing assumptions, Systems Thinking promotes a culture of innovation. It encourages teams to explore new perspectives and discover creative solutions to complex problems.

How Systems Thinking Works:

- **Identifying System Boundaries:** Systems Thinking begins by defining the boundaries of the system under consideration. This involves identifying the components, actors, and relationships that are relevant to the problem or issue being addressed.
- **Mapping Interconnections:** Once the system boundaries are defined, Systems Thinking involves mapping out the interconnections and relationships between different components within the system. This may include feedback loops, causal relationships, and dependencies that influence system behavior.
- **Understanding System Dynamics:** Systems Thinking seeks to understand the dynamic behavior of systems over time. This involves analyzing how changes in one part of the

system can ripple through interconnected components, leading to emergent behaviors and patterns.
- **Identifying Leverage Points:** Systems Thinking enables teams to identify leverage points within a system where small interventions can lead to significant changes. These leverage points may involve altering system structures, changing feedback loops, or shifting underlying mental models.
- **Anticipating Unintended Consequences:** Systems Thinking helps organizations anticipate potential unintended consequences of interventions by considering the broader system dynamics. By conducting system-wide impact assessments, organizations can identify potential risks and develop mitigation strategies to minimize negative outcomes.

By understanding why Systems Thinking matters and how it works, organizations can leverage this framework to tackle complex challenges, drive innovation, and create more sustainable and resilient systems.

How can I apply it on my team? Applying the Design for Strategy framework in your team involves practical steps to align design thinking with strategic goals. Let's explore how you can do this:

1. **Define the Problem:** Clearly articulate the issue your team is tackling. Map out the system's boundaries and understand the interconnected components and their relationships.

2. **Visualize the System:** Create diagrams such as causal loop diagrams or influence maps to depict the system's components, actors, and interactions. This helps visualize how elements influence one another.

3. **Analyze Feedback Loops:** Identify and understand feedback loops within the system—both positive and negative. Recognize how changes in one area can affect other parts through these loops.

4. **Examine Interconnections:** Explore how different components are interconnected. Assess the impact of changes in one component on others and the overall system.

5. **Find Leverage Points:** Pinpoint areas where small changes can have substantial effects. Leverage points could involve modifying system structures, adjusting feedback loops, or shifting mental models.

6. **Anticipate Unintended Consequences:** Consider potential ripple effects of interventions. Develop strategies to mitigate risks and address possible side effects on other components or stakeholders.

7. **Iterate and Adapt:** Embrace Systems Thinking as an iterative process. Encourage ongoing reflection, stakeholder feedback, and refinement of mental models and interventions based on new insights.

These steps will help your team apply the Design for Strategy framework effectively, fostering alignment between design thinking and strategic objectives.

What are some challenges that could be encountered during start-up?

Improving processes within Canadian public service organizations, especially through the implementation of methodologies like Systems Thinking, faces significant challenges rooted in the complexity and bureaucracy inherent in many government operations. One notable obstacle is the prevalence of lengthy and complex processes that characterize various aspects of public sector work. For instance, within Service Canada, responsible for delivering a wide range of citizen services, intricate procedures for accessing benefits or assistance can be overwhelming for both employees and service users (Service Canada, "Annual Report 2020-2021").

These complex processes hinder the effective implementation of Systems Thinking methodologies aimed at streamlining operations and enhancing service delivery. Moreover, the slow or clunky adoption of new processes further complicates improvement efforts within public service organizations. Operating within a risk-averse environment, characterized by adherence to established procedures and protocols, can impede the adoption of innovative methodologies. This inertia is particularly pronounced in organizations like the Department of National Defense (DND), where stringent security protocols and hierarchical structures contribute to resistance to change (DND, "Report on Plans and Priorities 2021-2022"). Overcoming this resistance requires proactive efforts to address stakeholder concerns, alleviate fears of disruption, and demonstrate the benefits of adopting Systems Thinking approaches.

In addressing these challenges, public service organizations must prioritize fostering a culture of continuous improvement and innovation. This involves not only streamlining processes but also cultivating an environment where experimentation and learning are encouraged. By promoting a mindset of adaptability and resilience, organizations can better navigate the complexities of implementing new methodologies like Systems Thinking, ultimately enhancing their ability to deliver value to citizens and stakeholders. Through effective change management strategies and a commitment to organizational learning, public service organizations can overcome barriers to process improvement and drive meaningful change in service delivery.

Related Literature on Systems Thinking:

- "The Fifth Discipline: The Art and Practice of the Learning Organization" by Peter M. Senge - This seminal book introduces the concept of Systems Thinking and its application in organizations. It offers practical guidance on how to cultivate a learning organization that can thrive in a complex and interconnected world.
- "Thinking in Systems: A Primer" by Donella H. Meadows - This book provides a concise introduction to Systems Thinking and its practical applications. Donella Meadows explores key concepts such as feedback loops, stocks and flows, and resilience, offering insights into how systems behave and how to intervene effectively.
- "Systems Thinking for Social Change: A Practical Guide to Solving Complex Problems, Avoiding Unintended Consequences, and Achieving Lasting Results" by David Peter Stroh - This practical guide offers tools and techniques for applying Systems Thinking to address complex social and environmental challenges. It provides real-world examples and case studies to illustrate how Systems Thinking can be used to achieve meaningful impact.
- "Thinking, Fast and Slow" by Daniel Kahneman - While not solely focused on Systems Thinking, this book explores the cognitive biases and heuristics that influence decision-making. Understanding these biases can help teams apply Systems Thinking more effectively by recognizing and mitigating cognitive traps.
- "Systems Thinking: Managing Chaos and Complexity: A Platform for Designing Business Architecture" by Jamshid Gharajedaghi - This book offers a comprehensive overview of Systems Thinking principles and practices, with a focus on their application in business architecture and organizational design. It provides practical frameworks and tools for managing complexity and driving organizational change.

These resources provide valuable insights and practical guidance for applying Systems Thinking principles and practices to your team's projects and initiatives.

6. Emotional Intelligence:

   Is tied to "Acknowledge you don't know everything" mindset.

   What it is. Emotional intelligence frameworks help leaders and teams understand and manage emotions effectively. By fostering self-awareness, empathy, and relationship management, teams can enhance communication, collaboration, and decision-making.

   Why Emotional Intelligence Matters:

   - **Enhanced Relationships:** Emotional Intelligence (EI) strengthens personal and professional connections by fostering self-awareness and empathy. This leads to deeper trust and more effective collaboration.
   - **Improved Communication:** EI enhances communication by promoting clear expression and active listening. It enables individuals to manage emotions during interactions, leading to more authentic exchanges, constructive conflict resolution, and greater empathy.
   - **Better Decision-Making:** By managing emotions like stress and bias, EI supports more rational and informed decision-making. It helps individuals balance logical reasoning with emotional insights, ensuring decisions align with values and goals.
   - **Increased Resilience:** EI boosts resilience by improving stress management and adaptive coping strategies. Individuals with high EI recover from setbacks faster, maintain a positive outlook, and navigate change with greater ease.
   - **Enhanced Leadership Effectiveness:** High EI is crucial for effective leadership, enabling leaders to inspire and motivate others. It helps leaders understand team needs, create a supportive environment, and lead authentically through emotional self-regulation.

   How Emotional Intelligence Works:

   - Self-Awareness: By developing self-awareness, individuals gain insight into their own emotions, strengths, and triggers, leading to better emotional management and more deliberate behavior choices.

- Self-Regulation: Mastering self-regulation allows individuals to manage emotions and impulses through techniques like deep breathing and mindfulness. This fosters greater composure, resilience, and adaptability in challenging situations.
- Empathy: Cultivating empathy enables individuals to understand and connect with others' emotions, fostering compassion and trust. This skill enhances communication and relationship-building by aligning behavior with others' needs.
- Social Skills: Strong social skills, including effective communication, collaboration, and conflict resolution, help individuals navigate interpersonal dynamics, build positive relationships, and influence others through persuasive and respectful interactions.
- Motivation: High motivation drives individuals to set ambitious goals, overcome obstacles, and pursue excellence. Motivated individuals maintain high standards and continuously seek opportunities for growth and achievement.

By understanding why Emotional Intelligence matters and how it works, individuals and teams can cultivate and leverage it to enhance their relationships, communication, decision-making, resilience, and leadership effectiveness.

7 Easy Steps to Apply Emotional Intelligence to your work teams:

1. Encourage reflection and self-assessment to help team members understand their emotions and behavior patterns.

2. Provide training in mindfulness and stress management to help team members stay composed and manage reactions effectively.

3. Foster active listening and understanding by creating opportunities for open sharing and team-building activities.

4. Offer training in communication, collaboration, and conflict resolution to improve interpersonal dynamics.

5. Align goals with personal values, celebrate achievements, and provide growth opportunities to keep team members engaged.

6. Demonstrate emotional intelligence through transparency, empathy, and feedback to build trust and inspire your team.

7. Support continuous learning by providing development resources and encouraging self-improvement.

What are some challenges that could be encountered during start-up?

Improving processes in Canadian public service organizations, particularly through the integration of new methodologies like Emotional Intelligence (EI), presents several challenges that require careful consideration and strategic intervention. One common obstacle is the presence of bureaucratic hurdles that stifle efficiency and hinder innovation. For instance, within the Department of Immigration, Refugees and Citizenship Canada (IRCC), responsible for managing immigration and refugee programs, bureaucratic structures and protocols can impede the adoption of EI principles among staff (IRCC, "Departmental Plan 2021-2022"). These rigid systems may inhibit teams from cultivating self-awareness, empathy, and relationship management skills, thereby hindering efforts to enhance service delivery and responsiveness.

Moreover, lengthy approval processes often plague public service organizations, further complicating the implementation of new ideas and solutions rooted in EI. These cumbersome procedures can delay the adoption of innovative approaches to service delivery, as decisions get caught in bureaucratic red tape. In organizations like the Canadian Food Inspection Agency (CFIA), tasked with ensuring the safety and quality of food products, lengthy approval processes may hinder timely responses to emerging food safety concerns or regulatory changes (CFIA, "Departmental Plan 2021-2022"). As a result, teams may struggle to foster a culture of empathy and collaboration, ultimately impacting their ability to meet the diverse needs of Canadians effectively.

To overcome these challenges, public service organizations must actively address the structural barriers and procedural inefficiencies that impede progress. This may involve streamlining approval processes, promoting transparency and accountability, and fostering a culture of continuous improvement and learning. By prioritizing Emotional Intelligence and addressing bureaucratic obstacles, public service organizations can enhance their ability to deliver responsive, empathetic, and effective services to the communities they serve. Through targeted interventions and a commitment to organizational development, public service organizations can navigate the complexities of implementing EI principles and drive meaningful improvements in service delivery.

Related Literature on Emotional Intelligence:

- "Emotional Intelligence: Why It Can Matter More Than IQ" by Daniel Goleman - This bestselling book provides an in-depth exploration of emotional intelligence and its impact on personal and professional success. Daniel Goleman explores the five components of EI and offers practical strategies for developing emotional intelligence skills.
- "The EQ Edge: Emotional Intelligence and Your Success" by Steven J. Stein and Howard E. Book - This comprehensive guide offers practical tools and techniques for assessing and developing emotional intelligence in individuals and teams. It includes self-assessment tools, case studies, and exercises to help readers enhance their EI skills and achieve greater success.
- "Primal Leadership: Realizing the Power of Emotional Intelligence" by Daniel Goleman, Richard E. Boyatzis, and Annie McKee - This book explores the role of emotional intelligence in effective leadership. Drawing on research and real-world examples, the

authors demonstrate how leaders can leverage emotional intelligence to inspire and motivate others, build high-performing teams, and drive organizational success.
- "The Emotionally Intelligent Team: Understanding and Developing the Behaviors of Success" by Marcia Hughes, Henry L. Thompson, and James Bradford Terrell - This book explores the dynamics of emotional intelligence within teams and offers practical guidance for building emotionally intelligent teams. It includes assessments, exercises, and case studies to help teams develop their EI skills and achieve greater cohesion and effectiveness.

These resources offer key insights and actionable advice for integrating emotional intelligence principles into your team's dynamics and enhancing performance.

7. Design for Strategy:

It connects to "Think critically about your choices" mindset.

What it is: The Design for Strategy framework focuses on making strategic choices that align and reinforce each other, setting the stage for organizational success. By integrating design thinking with strategic goals, teams can craft innovative solutions that drive growth and secure a competitive advantage. This approach, championed by Tim Brown of IDEO[38], highlights how incorporating design thinking into strategy development fosters more effective and creative decision-making.

Why it matters: The Design for Strategy framework provides a structured approach to strategic decision-making, ensuring alignment and integration. In a rapidly changing business environment, it helps organizations tackle immediate challenges and secure long-term success. By applying design thinking, organizations foster innovation, creativity, and customer focus, enabling them to uncover new opportunities, anticipate trends, and maintain a competitive edge.

How it works: The framework guides teams in defining strategic choices, designing integrated solutions, and aligning resources. It begins with analyzing the current position and market dynamics, then identifies key strategic choices that interconnect to form a cohesive strategy. Using design thinking, teams iterate on these choices, prototype, and test solutions. Continuous monitoring and feedback ensure the strategy remains agile and responsive to change.

How can I apply it on my team? Applying the Design for Strategy framework in your team involves 7 practical steps to align design thinking with strategic goals. Let's explore how you can do this:

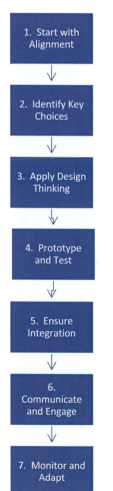

1. Ensure your team fully understands the organization's mission, vision, and strategic objectives. Align everyone around common goals to create a unified sense of purpose.

2. Collaborate with your team to identify and interconnect key strategic choices, forming a cohesive strategy that supports your objectives.

3. Apply design thinking principles to explore and develop innovative solutions. Foster creativity, empathy, and experimentation to uncover new opportunities.

4. Create and test prototypes of your solutions with stakeholders, including customers and partners. Use their feedback to iteratively refine and enhance your ideas.

5. Integrate strategic choices and solutions across all functions and levels. Aim for synergy and coherence in resource allocation and coordination of activities.

6. Clearly communicate the strategic direction and rationale to your team and stakeholders. Promote active involvement to build ownership and commitment to the strategy.

7. Continuously track performance and market trends to evaluate your strategy's effectiveness. Be ready to adapt and pivot based on new conditions and opportunities.

What are some challenges that could be encountered when implementing this?

Improving processes in Canadian public service organizations, particularly when integrating new methodologies such as Design for Strategy, encounters several challenges deeply rooted in bureaucratic structures. Bureaucratic hurdles often emerge as a significant barrier, impeding efficiency and stifling innovation. For instance, within the Canada Revenue Agency (CRA), responsible for tax administration and revenue collection, bureaucratic complexities may slow down decision-making processes, hindering the adoption of innovative strategies (CRA, "Departmental Plan 2021-2022"). The "Departmental Plan" outlines the strategic priorities and initiatives undertaken by the CRA to improve service delivery and operational effectiveness. It highlights the challenges posed by bureaucratic hurdles and the agency's commitment to streamlining processes to enhance efficiency and innovation.

Moreover, lengthy approval processes further exacerbate these challenges, leading to delays in adopting new ideas and solutions. In the context of public service organizations like Service Canada, tasked with delivering a wide range of citizen services, lengthy approval processes may impede timely responses to emerging needs or changes in service delivery models (Service Canada, "Departmental Plan 2021-2022"). The "Departmental Plan" provides insights into Service Canada's efforts to enhance service delivery and improve client experiences, including initiatives aimed at streamlining approval processes and reducing bureaucratic delays.

Addressing these challenges requires a concerted effort to reform entrenched bureaucratic practices and streamline approval processes. Public service organizations must cultivate a culture that values agility, innovation, and responsiveness to changing needs. This may involve restructuring organizational hierarchies, empowering frontline employees to make decisions, and implementing agile project management methodologies. Additionally, investing in technology and digital transformation initiatives can help automate repetitive tasks and streamline workflows, reducing the burden of bureaucratic inefficiencies. Through strategic initiatives outlined in departmental plans and supported by strong leadership and stakeholder engagement, public service organizations can overcome bureaucratic hurdles and drive sustainable process improvements to better serve Canadians.

Consulting Case Study #3:

To demonstrate the application of the Design for Strategy framework, I will refer to the Ministry client discussed in the Design Thinking section. After initially assisting them with service delivery modernization, I was re-engaged to enhance their future strategic planning. The goal was to build on the existing framework to improve strategic planning and ensure ongoing service delivery enhancements.

I began by ensuring the team had a deep understanding of the Ministry's mission, vision, and strategic objectives, aligning everyone around these common goals to create a unified purpose. We then identified and interconnected key strategic choices, developing a cohesive strategy based on the Design for Strategy methodology.

Using design thinking principles, we fostered creativity through brainstorming and mind mapping, developing prototypes of promising ideas. These prototypes were tested with stakeholders, and feedback was used to iteratively refine the solutions.

The project led to several significant outcomes:

1. Enhanced Strategic Planning Framework: A refined framework integrated human-centered design with the Ministry's strategic objectives, providing a structured approach to planning and execution.
2. Improved Resource Allocation: The cohesive strategy facilitated more effective resource allocation, leading to better coordination and operational efficiency.
3. Increased Innovation and Responsiveness: Design thinking principles encouraged creativity and experimentation, making the Ministry more adaptable to emerging trends and challenges.
4. Strengthened Stakeholder Engagement: Prototyping and testing with stakeholders ensured practical, user-centered solutions and strengthened stakeholder relationships.
5. Ongoing Strategic Agility: The framework included mechanisms for continuous monitoring and adaptation, ensuring the Ministry remained agile and responsive to evolving needs and market conditions.

Overall, the project significantly enhanced the Ministry's strategic planning, resource allocation, innovation, stakeholder engagement, and agility in service delivery and modernization efforts.

Related Literature:

- "Playing to Win: How Strategy Really Works" by A.G. Lafley and Roger L. Martin: This book provides insights into strategic decision-making and offers a practical framework for developing winning strategies.
- "The Design of Business: Why Design Thinking is the Next Competitive Advantage" by Roger L. Martin: In this book, Martin explores the role of design thinking in driving innovation and creating value in business.
- "The Opposable Mind: How Successful Leaders Win Through Integrative Thinking" by Roger L. Martin: This book introduces the concept of integrative thinking and demonstrates how leaders can use it to tackle complex problems and make better decisions.
- "Creating Great Choices: A Leader's Guide to Integrative Thinking" by Jennifer Riel and Roger L. Martin: This book provides practical guidance on how to apply integrative thinking to generate innovative solutions and navigate strategic challenges effectively.
- Roger Martin's book "Creating Great Choices: A Leader's Guide to Integrative Thinking" where he discusses the application of the Design for Strategy framework in various sectors, including government services.)

8. The Coaching Mindset Approach:

It aligns with the question: "How can I empower my staff *vs* just managing them?"

What it is. The Coaching Mindset approach extends beyond merely applying coaching techniques; it involves adopting a comprehensive philosophy that champions continuous learning, employee empowerment, and a nurturing environment for growth.

By integrating coaching frameworks like the **GROW model** and the **Solution Focused model**, leaders can enhance their effectiveness. The GROW model[39], developed by Sir John Whitmore from the UK and popularized in his 1992 book "Coaching for Performance," helps in setting goals and finding actionable steps. The Solution Focused model[40], created by

Steve de Shazer and Insoo Kim Berg from the USA in the late 1980s, emphasizes leveraging strengths and resources to build solutions rather than fixating on problems.

In practical terms, this approach involves asking insightful questions that focus on desired futures and harness existing strengths. For example, the so-called **Miracle Question**—"Imagine that while you are asleep, a miracle occurs, and your current challenges are resolved. What will be the first sign that indicates a positive change has occurred?"—helps clients visualize and articulate their ideal future. **Scaling Questions**—"On a scale from 0 to 10 (where 0 represents the problem being at its worst and 10 means the problem is completely resolved), where do you currently stand?"—encourage clients to assess their progress and identify actionable steps to advance. Additionally, **Resource-Oriented Questions**—"What strengths or resources do you have that could help you in this situation?"—help clients identify and utilize their own assets. These are some of the questions that focus toward solutions and progress, not on why we are in this situation, fostering a proactive and positive mindset.

On the other hand, there is also the so-called **GROWTH mindset**[41]—the belief that abilities can be developed through dedication. This mindset encourages embracing challenges, persistent effort, learning from criticism, inspiring others, achieving higher results, and enhancing well-being.

With all this in mind, I began to explore what could happen if we integrate these concepts with my C.H.A.N.G.E. Framework© introducing at the same time a sense of urgency by delimiting a specific time horizon. This led me to create the GROWth Mindset Approach©, which effectively combines these powerful frameworks and emphasizes timely execution to drive transformative and measurable outcomes. The following visual demonstrates how these elements integrate seamlessly.

Exhibit #12

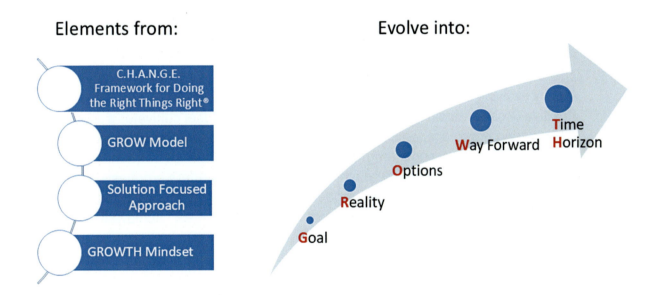

Here's why it Matters:

- **Holistic Development:** Integrating the GROW and Solution Focused models with a growth mindset creates a holistic approach to personal and professional development. This strategy not only addresses immediate issues but also embeds continuous learning and growth into the organizational culture.
- **Empowerment and Autonomy:** This framework empowers individuals to take charge of their own development by focusing on internal motivation rather than external validation. It fosters a sense of autonomy and control over personal growth.
- **Resilience and Adaptability:** The GROWth Mindset Approach© helps individuals view challenges as opportunities for growth, enhancing their resilience and adaptability in a rapidly evolving environment.
- **Positive Organizational Impact:** Adopting a coaching mindset cultivates a supportive and empowering workplace, which enhances individual well-being, improves team dynamics, boosts collaboration, and strengthens overall organizational performance.
- **Sustainable Success:** This approach blends the GROW model's emphasis on actionable steps with the Solution-Focused model's strengths-based approach, creating a solid foundation for enduring success. It promotes setting clear, achievable goals while harnessing personal strengths to reach long-term objectives.
- **Cultural Shift:** Implementing this framework can drive a cultural transformation within an organization or community. It fosters a culture of empathy, mutual support, and shared commitment to growth, fundamentally improving interactions and teamwork.

In essence, adopting The **GROWth Solution Mindset Coaching©** fosters a leadership culture rooted in growth and human development. It cultivates a collaborative environment where growth becomes a shared goal, resulting in more impactful and meaningful outcomes. The visual below displays how these elements work together seamlessly.

Exhibit #13

The GROWth Solution Mindset Coaching©

This is how it works: The visual illustrates that fostering a growth-oriented environment begins with defining a compelling vision, or **"Winning Aspiration,"** that aligns with the team's collective goals. This vision serves as a North Star, guiding the team from their current state to their desired future. Following this, it's essential to **assess the team's current reality**, identifying strengths and areas for improvement while establishing a supportive network to drive progress.

With a solid grasp of the **starting point** and **end goals**, engage the team in exploring various strategies to reach their objectives. Set **Inspirational Goals** that challenge and motivate the team and **develop Time-Bound Action Plans** that outline specific, measurable steps with clear deadlines. **Empower team members to implement these plans**, ensuring everyone understands their roles and responsibilities. As plans unfold, leaders should support, monitor progress, and foster a feedback-rich environment that encourages continuous adaptation and growth.

Following this approach not only accelerates goal achievement but also nurtures a resilient, collaborative, and success-driven team culture.

These would be the steps to follow:

6 Easy Steps to apply the GROWth Solution Mindset Coaching© framework:

1. Reflect on your current position and where you want to go. This clarity on 'What' and 'Why' sets a purposeful direction for your journey.

2. A critical look at the present situation helps to establish a baseline. Building a strong network ensures you have the necessary support and resources. This network acts as a sounding board and a source of guidance as you navigate your growth.

3. Understand available options. Identify and evaluate all possible pathways to bridge the gap between your current situation and your aspirations and choose the best route to success.

4. Goals should inspire action and motivate continuous progress. By shifting the focus from problems to solutions, you create a positive and proactive framework that encourages forward-thinking and innovation.

5. Action plans need to be Specific, Measurable, and Time-bound. This SMART framework ensures that goals are not just aspirational but also attainable, with clear metrics for tracking progress.

6. Implementation is where plans come to life. Monitoring progress and adapting strategies as needed are essential. Encouraging responsiveness to feedback and results helps maintain momentum and ensures alignment with the winning aspiration.

What could be the possible challenges when implementing the GROWth Solution Mindset Coaching© framework?

Let's talk about the Canadian Public Sector in particular:

- **Complexity and Change:** The public sector in Canada is grappling with complex challenges such as digital innovation, labor shortages, climate change, and social issues

like structural racism. These external forces demand a leadership style that is adaptive and innovative.
- **Bureaucratic Inertia:** Traditional methods of policy planning and implementation may not align well with the agile and flexible nature of coaching. There's a need for a shift from long-term planning to more dynamic and responsive decision-making.
- **Cultural Shift:** Adopting a coaching mindset requires a significant cultural shift. Public sector organizations often have established cultures that may resist the changes necessary to implement a coaching approach effectively.
- **Leadership Development:** There is a growing recognition of the need for a growth mindset and committed coaching, but few public sector organizations have fully integrated these into a unified leadership model. Developing leaders who can coach and empower their teams is essential.
- **Resource Allocation:** Implementing a coaching mindset approach may require additional resources, such as training and development programs, which can be challenging to secure in the public sector.
- **Measuring Impact:** The benefits of a coaching mindset, such as increased employee engagement and well-being, can be difficult to measure and may not be immediately apparent, making it challenging to demonstrate the value of the approach.

Addressing these challenges requires a concerted effort to develop leaders who can navigate these complexities and foster an environment conducive to any sort of coaching mindset approach. I'm not saying it's easy, but it's certainly possible. In fact, below I share successful case studies of a coaching mindset implementation in the Canadian Public Sector.

A couple of examples comes to mind:

As an Executive Coach, I have successfully introduced the GROWth Solution Mindset Coaching© Framework to various executive clients. In one notable project, I guided a federal department through a digital transformation by helping executives envision a digital-forward future, assess technological capabilities, and identify growth opportunities. We set inspirational goals and created actionable plans that the executives implemented with their teams, fostering a culture of continuous feedback and adaptation.

In another project, I tackled structural racism within a provincial government agency by first aligning with the executive team's diversity and inclusion goals. I introduced the GROWth Solution Mindset Coaching© Framework and worked with them to develop and implement a comprehensive inclusivity strategy. This strategy included initiatives such as bias training and mentorship programs, which were rolled out under executive leadership. By creating a supportive environment, we were able to track the impact of these initiatives and make necessary adjustments, showcasing the framework's.

Finally, in my role as a strategic advisor, I introduced the GROWth Solution Mindset Coaching© Framework to the executive team of a Crown corporation undergoing significant restructuring. We started by creating a shared vision that turned the restructuring into an opportunity for innovation and growth. I guided the team in assessing the corporation's structure to identify areas for increased efficiency and better alignment with strategic objectives.co

We developed a comprehensive plan with inspirational goals aimed at shifting focus from restructuring challenges to the potential benefits. I collaborated with the executives to create detailed action plans that were specific, measurable, and time bound. As these plans were rolled out, I supported the executives in fostering a culture of open communication and feedback. This approach enabled us to monitor progress and adapt strategies in real-time, ensuring effective navigation of the restructuring while upholding a commitment to service excellence and public accountability.

I hope these examples illustrate what can be achieved at any given time by applying the GROWth Solution Mindset Coaching© Framework to guide public organizations through periods of transformation, ensuring that actions are not only effective but also align with the principles of growth and continuous improvement.

Related Literature:

- Generative Leadership in Canada's Public Sector | BCG Canada. https://www.bcg.com/publications/2022/generative-leadership-aiding-canadas-public-sector.
- Coaching and Leadership in the Public Sector - Westminster Insight. https://www.westminsterinsight.com/insights/coaching-and-leadership-in-the-public-sector/.

- Promoting an Experimental Problem-Solving Mindset among Public Servants. https://unpan.un.org/sites/default/files/d8-files/Changing%20mindsets%20report%20-%20chapter4.pdf.
- Why Executive Coaching Makes Sense in the Public Sector. https://johnmattone.com/blog/why-executive-coaching-makes-sense-in-the-public-sector/
- Peer Coaching in Government: A set of Case Studies. By William Bergquist, Jennifer Ellis, et al. The International Journal of Coaching in Organizations
- Kutsyuruba, B. and Godden, L. (2019), "The role of mentoring and coaching as a means of supporting the well-being of educators and students", International Journal of Mentoring and Coaching in Education, Vol. 8 No. 4, pp. 229-234. https://doi.org/10.1108/IJMCE-12-2019-081

Transforming Outcomes Using These Proven Frameworks.

The following real-life references illustrate how these tried and tested frameworks can lead to significant improvements in processes, products, and services:

1. Lean Principles:

Worldwide: *Toyota* serves as a prominent exemplar of Lean Principles application. Through the introduction of the Just-in-Time system, they markedly diminished waste and bolstered efficiency within their production processes. (For more information, refer to "The Toyota Way: 14 Management Principles from the World's Greatest Manufacturer" by Jeffrey K. Liker)

Canadian Public Sector: The **Government of Canada** implemented Lean Principles throughout its departments. One example is the *Atlantic Canada Opportunities Agency*'s investment in training for employees to engage in a Lean Six Sigma methodology, with the purpose of improving internal business processes and ensuring continuous development1. (https://oecd-opsi.org/blog/implementing-lean-principles-throughout-the-government-of-canada/)

2. Design Thinking:

Worldwide: *IBM* exemplifies successful utilization of design thinking to overhaul their enterprise strategies and align more closely with user demands. The formulation of the IBM Design Thinking framework has fostered the creation of products and services centered around human needs. (For further insights, consult "Creative Confidence: Unleashing the Creative Potential Within Us All" by Tom Kelley and David Kelley).

Canadian Public Sector: The **Canadian public service** has been using design thinking to modernize products and services in a way that is both innovative and effective. For instance, design thinking has been applied to retrofitting housing developments for net zero carbon emissions, reducing patient relapses in an integrated health care system, and improving the experience of creating Government of Canada forms. (https://busrides-trajetsenbus.csps-efpc.gc.ca/en/ep-98-en)

3. Agile Practices:

Worldwide: *Spotify* stands out as a notable instance of Agile methodology implementation. Through the adoption of squads, tribes, chapters, and guilds, they maintain agility, swiftly adapting to changes and consistently delivering value to their clientele. (For deeper understanding, dive into "Scrum: The Art of Doing Twice the Work in Half the Time" by Jeff Sutherland).

Canadian Public Sector: The *Canadian Digital Service (CDS)* adopted Agile practices to develop and launch digital government services, such as the Canada.ca website, in iterative phases, allowing for continuous feedback and rapid adjustments to meet user needs effectively. (https://digital.canada.ca/2022/06/08/moving-fast-staying-safe-being-agile-in-government/)

4. Change Management:

Worldwide: *Procter & Gamble* effectively applied change management principles during their transition from a product-centric to a consumer-centric organizational structure. This substantial reconfiguration was adeptly managed and communicated, resulting in heightened profits and market dominance. (For detailed analysis, refer to "Leading Change" by John P. Kotter.)

Canadian Public Sector: The *Canadian public service* has undertaken major change initiatives to modernize programs and services. For instance, the *Privy Council Office* acknowledged the key role that career development can play in building equitable and rewarding workplaces for public servants. (https://articles.alpha.canada.ca/framework-for-leading-change/leading-change-in-government/)

5. Systems Thinking:

The **World Health Organization** harnessed systems thinking to enhance global health initiatives. By scrutinizing the intricate interplay between various health systems, they successfully implemented more impactful and sustainable health interventions. (For a comprehensive perspective, consult "Thinking in Systems: A Primer" by Donella H. Meadows).

Canadian Public Sector: The **Department of Fisheries and Oceans (DFO)** in Canada has successfully integrated systems thinking into its management strategies, as detailed in the case study "Fisheries and Oceans Canada's Ecosystem Approach to Fisheries Management Working Group: Case Study Synthesis and Lessons Learned." This approach has enhanced decision-making and management effectiveness.

(Pepin, Pierre, et al. Fisheries and Oceans Canada's Ecosystem Approach to Fisheries Management Working Group: Case Study Synthesis and Lessons Learned. Fisheries and Oceans Canada, Northwest Atlantic Fisheries Centre, 2023. Web. https://publications.gc.ca/site/eng/9.924612/publication.html.)

6. Emotional Intelligence:

Worldwide: *Google's* "Project Aristotle" uncovered the pivotal role of emotional intelligence in team success. This revelation prompted the implementation of emotional intelligence training and development initiatives. (To delve deeper, explore "Emotional Intelligence 2.0" by Travis Bradberry and Jean Greaves).

Canadian Public Sector: The **Canadian School of Public Service** offers a job aid that provides practical tips on how to lead with emotional intelligence and encourage effective and emotionally healthy teams. (https://www.csps-efpc.gc.ca/tools/jobaids/emotional-intelligence-eng.aspx)

The *Royal Canadian Mounted Police (RCMP)* has implemented emotional intelligence training programs for their frontline officers. A study titled "Assessing the impact of the *Royal Canadian Mounted Police (RCMP)* protocol and Emotional Resilience Skills Training (ERST) among diverse public safety personnel" discusses this initiative. (Haight, M. (2022). Assessing the impact of the Royal Canadian Mounted Police (RCMP) BMC Psychology https://bmcpsychology.biomedcentral.com)

7. Design for Strategy:

Worldwide: *Airbnb* utilized strategic design principles to revolutionize their business model. By reconceptualizing the entire user journey, they distinguished themselves in the market and achieved remarkable growth. (For further exploration, refer to "Design a Better Business: New Tools, Skills, and Mindset for Strategy and Innovation" by Patrick Van Der Pijl, Justin Lokitz, and Lisa Solomon).

Canadian Public Sector:

Canadian Public Sector: *ServiceOntario* utilized the Design for Strategy framework to redesign its online service portal, making it more user-friendly and intuitive for citizens accessing government services digitally. By employing design thinking principles and incorporating user feedback iteratively, *ServiceOntario* aimed to streamline processes and improve the overall user experience. (Source: ServiceOntario: Redesigning the Online Service Portal. (n.d.). Retrieved from https://www.ontario.ca/page/serviceontario).

The **Government of Canada** adopted the Design for Strategy framework to develop and implement its Digital Service Strategy, aimed at modernizing digital service delivery across federal departments and agencies. One aspect of the strategy involved the creation of a centralized digital platform where Canadians could access government services and information in a seamless and user-centric manner. By applying design thinking principles and iterative development processes, the government sought to improve accessibility, usability, and efficiency in delivering digital services to citizens. (Source: The Government of Canada's Digital Ambition: 2022–23 Year in Review https://www.canada.ca/en/government/system/digital-government/digital-ambition/2022-2023-year-in-review.html)

Bottom line:

By leveraging these frameworks and best practices, teams can benefit from established methodologies and approaches that have been proven effective in various contexts. Rather than starting from scratch, teams can build upon existing knowledge and expertise, accelerating problem-solving efforts and increasing the likelihood of successful outcomes. Additionally, these frameworks provide a common language and set of tools that facilitate collaboration and alignment among team members, further enhancing the problem-solving process.

Some tricks of the trade for adopting new frameworks

Drawing from my years of experience in implementing frameworks to streamline complex processes and achieve consistent, effective outcomes, I've identified key strategies that ensure smoother adoption. These proven approaches, or 'tricks of the trade,' can enhance integration and maximize the benefits of innovative frameworks in your work. Here are the main takeaways:

A. Prioritizing Frameworks: Understanding What Matters Most

Before diving into framework implementation, public service organizations in Canada should first identify which frameworks best align with their goals and needs. Here's how to ensure a successful integration:

1. Understand Business Needs: Begin by clarifying the organization's overarching goals and challenges. This foundational understanding helps pinpoint which frameworks can effectively address specific obstacles.
2. Assess Current State: Evaluate existing processes and identify areas for improvement. This insight helps in selecting frameworks that complement and enhance current operations.
3. Research Frameworks: Investigate various frameworks to find those that offer solutions tailored to your organization's challenges. Examine each framework's specifics to ensure a good fit.
4. Consider Resource Availability: Ensure the organization has the necessary resources, including budget and skills, to successfully implement the chosen frameworks.
5. Evaluate Potential Impact: Weigh the benefits and costs of each framework. Assessing the potential impact helps prioritize frameworks that offer the most significant advantages.
6. Pilot Frameworks: Conduct small-scale tests to gauge the effectiveness of the frameworks in practice. This approach allows for adjustments before a full-scale rollout.
7. Seek External Advice: Consult with experts and other organizations that have implemented similar frameworks. External insights can offer valuable guidance and enhance decision-making.

 By following these steps, public service organizations can strategically select and implement frameworks that deliver maximum value and align with their specific needs, ensuring a more effective and impactful transformation.

B. Ensuring Staff Buy-in: Getting Everyone on Board

Implementing a new framework goes beyond selecting the right one; it's crucial to secure staff commitment. Here's how organizations can effectively engage their teams:

1. Early Involvement and Communication: Engage staff from the start by clearly explaining the purpose and benefits of the framework. Involving them in decision-making helps them understand their role and fosters support.
2. Education and Training: Provide comprehensive training to equip staff with the necessary skills and knowledge. This preparation ensures they can effectively implement the framework and contribute to its success.
3. Clear Expectations and Benefits: Define roles and outline how staff will benefit from the changes. Clear expectations and an understanding of personal benefits help motivate and align staff efforts.
4. Incentives and Recognition: Recognize and reward those who embrace the framework. Acknowledging their contributions and linking adoption to performance evaluations can encourage others to follow suit.
5. Addressing Concerns and Resistance: Proactively address any concerns or resistance through effective change management practices. This approach smooths the transition and reduces barriers to acceptance.
6. Peer Influence and Social Proof: Leverage positive experiences from early adopters. Encouraging staff to share success stories can build momentum and inspire others to engage with the framework.
7. Ownership and Empowerment: Give staff a sense of ownership by involving them in decision-making and encouraging creative application of the framework. Empowered staff are more committed and invested in the change process.

Remember, securing staff buy-in is an ongoing effort that requires active engagement and a supportive culture. When staff feel valued and see the framework's positive impact, their commitment and involvement will strengthen, driving overall success.

C. Measuring Staff Satisfaction: Keeping Tabs on How Everyone's Doing.

Once a framework is implemented and staff are on board, it's important to check in regularly to see how everyone's feeling about the changes. Here's how organizations can measure staff satisfaction:

1. Surveys and Feedback: Hearing Directly from the Team

Regular surveys and feedback sessions provide valuable insights into how staff are feeling about the framework. Anonymous surveys can encourage honest feedback, while open discussions allow for more in-depth conversations.

2. User Experience Metrics: Observing How Things Are Going

Observing staff as they use the framework in their day-to-day work can provide valuable insights into how well it's working in practice. Paying attention to things like usability and task completion time can help identify areas for improvement.

3. Adoption Rate and Engagement: Tracking Who's Getting on Board

Keeping an eye on how many staff are actively using the framework and engaging with its features can give a good indication of overall satisfaction. High adoption rates and engagement levels are typically a positive sign.

4. Support Requests and Tickets: Spotting Potential Pain Points

Analyzing helpdesk data can provide valuable insights into any issues or challenges staff are encountering. Frequent support requests may indicate areas where additional training is needed.

5. Focus Groups and Interviews: Going Deeper into the Issues

Organizing focus groups or conducting one-on-one interviews allows organizations to delve deeper into staff experiences and perspectives. These more qualitative methods can provide valuable context and help identify root causes of any dissatisfaction.

6. Comparative Analysis: Seeing How They Stack Up

Comparing staff satisfaction levels before and after framework implementation can provide valuable insights into its impact. Benchmarking against similar organizations can also help identify areas for improvement.

7. Employee Net Promoter Score: Gauging Overall Sentiment

The Employee Net Promoter Score (eNPS) measures how likely staff are to recommend the framework to others. It's calculated by asking employees to rate, on a scale from 0 to 10, how likely they are to promote the framework. Scores are then categorized into promoters, passives, and detractors. A high eNPS indicates that employees are satisfied and supportive, reflecting a positive overall sentiment.

8. Behavioral Indicators: Watching for Signs of Engagement

Finally, paying attention to staff behavior can provide valuable insights into their level of satisfaction. Staff who voluntarily adopt the framework and actively promote it to others are likely to be more satisfied with the changes.

Key Takeaway: Consistently monitoring staff satisfaction is essential for ensuring the framework aligns with their needs and supports organizational success. By combining quantitative metrics with qualitative insights, organizations can make informed adjustments, ensuring the framework evolves with staff preferences and maximizes its impact.

D. Ensuring Alignment with Existing Processes: Making Sure Everything Fits Together.

Implementing a new framework involves more than just selection—it's about ensuring it integrates smoothly with existing processes. Here's how organizations can achieve seamless alignment:

1. Understanding Existing Processes: Laying the Groundwork

Gain a thorough understanding of current processes by documenting them, pinpointing pain points, and defining desired outcomes. This foundational knowledge is crucial for effective integration.

2. Mapping Framework to Process: Connecting the dots

Align the new framework with existing processes by identifying overlaps and necessary adjustments. This ensures that the framework complements and enhances current operations rather than disrupting them.

3. Involving Stakeholders: Building Support

Engage all relevant stakeholders early in the process. Their input and buy-in are essential for successful alignment and implementation, ensuring that the framework meets the needs of those affected.

4. Piloting the Changes: Validating Integration

Conduct small-scale pilots to test the integration of aligned processes. This approach helps identify potential issues and make necessary adjustments before a full-scale rollout.

5. Clear and Consistent Communication: Keeping Everyone Informed

Maintain open lines of communication throughout the alignment process. Ensure that all team members understand the reasons for changes and how these changes will impact their work.

6. Providing Training: Ensuring Readiness

Offer comprehensive training to equip staff with the skills and knowledge needed to adapt to the new framework. Well-trained employees are better prepared to embrace changes and contribute to successful integration.

7. Regular Review and Adjustment: Ensuring Ongoing Success

Continuously monitor and review the alignment process. Collect feedback, assess performance metrics, and adjust as needed to ensure that the framework remains effective and aligned with existing processes.

Key Takeaway: Effective alignment of a new framework with existing processes is not a one-time event, it is an ongoing effort. By understanding current processes, involving stakeholders, piloting changes, and maintaining clear communication, organizations can ensure smooth integration and enhance overall efficiency.

E. Measuring Success of Alignment Efforts: Checking in to See How Things Are Going.

Once the framework is implemented and processes are aligned, it's important to measure the success of these efforts. Here's how organizations can do that:

1. Key Performance Indicators (KPIs): Tracking Progress Toward Goals

Identifying key performance indicators related to the alignment efforts allows organizations to track progress and assess impact. This might include metrics related to efficiency, quality, customer satisfaction, and financial performance.

2. Benchmarking: Seeing How They Stack Up

Comparing performance against industry benchmarks and best practices provides valuable context and helps organizations identify areas for improvement.

3. Feedback Gathering: Hearing from Those on the Front Lines

Regularly gathering feedback from staff and other stakeholders allows organizations to understand how well the aligned processes are working in practice and identify any areas for improvement.

4. Audits and Reviews: Keeping Things in Check

Conducting regular audits and reviews helps ensure that processes remain aligned over time and allows organizations to identify any deviations or areas for improvement.

5. Project Success Metrics: Assessing Overall Impact

Evaluating the success of alignment efforts against predefined project success metrics allows organizations to determine whether they've achieved their goals and objectives.

6. Employee Engagement and Satisfaction: Ensuring Everyone's on Board

Monitoring employee engagement and satisfaction levels allows organizations to gauge how well staff have embraced the changes and whether they feel supported and empowered in their roles.

Key Takeaway: Regularly measuring the success of alignment efforts ensures that processes remain effective and aligned with organizational goals. By using KPIs, benchmarking, feedback, audits, success metrics, and monitoring employee satisfaction, organizations can stay on track, make informed adjustments, and continuously improve their integration efforts.

Section Wrap-up

These steps offer a comprehensive roadmap for organizations to effectively prioritize, implement, and evaluate frameworks while ensuring staff engagement and alignment with existing processes. By following this approach, organizations can enhance their chances of success and achieve their goals more efficiently.

Remember, successful alignment requires a multifaceted strategy. A holistic approach that integrates quantitative metrics, qualitative feedback, and overall organizational impact ensures sustained commitment and ongoing improvement. Regularly revisiting these steps will help maintain momentum and drive continuous enhancement.

Recommended Reading:

In the context of public service organizations in Canada, here are some literature recommendations for the provided topics:

1. **How can organizations prioritize which frameworks to implement?**

- "Choosing the Right Prioritization Framework" by Adam Hale and Chip Heath: This article provides insights into various prioritization frameworks and offers guidance on selecting the most suitable one based on organizational needs and objectives.

- "Lean Enterprise: How High-Performance Organizations Innovate at Scale" by Jez Humble, Joanne Molesky, and Barry O'Reilly: This book explores strategies for prioritizing initiatives and frameworks within large organizations, drawing on principles from Lean and Agile methodologies.

- "Strategic Planning for Public and Nonprofit Organizations: A Guide to Strengthening and Sustaining Organizational Achievement" by John M. Bryson - This book offers insights into strategic planning processes tailored to public and nonprofit organizations. It provides frameworks for identifying strategic priorities and aligning organizational objectives with available resources, which can help inform decisions on which frameworks to prioritize.

- "Decision Making in Public Policy and Administration: A Handbook for Local Government" by Lloyd G. Nigro and Frank J. Montoya Jr. - This handbook explores decision-making processes within public organizations, offering guidance on prioritizing initiatives and allocating resources effectively. It provides practical strategies for evaluating the potential impact of different frameworks and selecting those that best align with organizational goals and priorities.

2. **How can organizations ensure alignment between the chosen frameworks and their existing processes?**

- "Enterprise Architecture as Strategy: Creating a Foundation for Business Execution" by Jeanne W. Ross, Peter Weill, and David Robertson: This book delves into the importance of aligning enterprise architecture with business strategy and processes, offering practical insights and frameworks for achieving alignment.

- "ITIL® Practitioner Guidance" by AXELOS: This publication provides guidance on adopting and adapting the ITIL framework to align IT service management practices with organizational goals and processes.

- "Aligning Frameworks and Processes in Public Administration: A Practice-Based Approach to Performance Management" by J. Michael Keegan and Eva K. Lee - This book examines the challenges of aligning frameworks and processes in public administration and offers practical strategies for achieving alignment. It discusses methods for assessing organizational processes, identifying areas for improvement, and integrating new frameworks effectively.

- "Managing Organizational Alignment: Strategic Alignment in Practice" by Danny Samson and Ron Beckett - This book explores the concept of organizational alignment and provides insights into how public sector organizations can align frameworks with existing processes to improve performance. It offers case studies and practical examples of successful alignment efforts, along with strategies for overcoming common barriers.

3. How can organizations measure the success of alignment efforts?

- "The Balanced Scorecard: Translating Strategy into Action" by Robert S. Kaplan and David P. Norton: This seminal work introduces the balanced scorecard framework for measuring organizational performance and aligning strategic objectives with key performance indicators (KPIs).

- "Measuring the Success of Change: A Step-by-Step Guide for Measuring the Impact and ROI in Change Management" by Stacy Aaron and Mark A. Smith: This book offers practical methods and tools for measuring the success of organizational change efforts, including alignment initiatives, using metrics and analytics.

- "Performance Measurement for Public and Nonprofit Organizations" by Theodore H. Poister - This book offers guidance on developing performance measurement systems tailored to public and nonprofit organizations. It discusses methods for evaluating the effectiveness of alignment efforts and measuring the impact on organizational performance.

- "Measuring the Success of Leadership Development: A Step-by-Step Guide for Measuring Impact and Calculating ROI" by Patricia Pulliam Phillips and Jack J. Phillips - While focused on leadership development, this book provides valuable insights into measuring the impact of organizational initiatives. It offers practical techniques for assessing alignment between frameworks and processes and determining the return on investment in alignment efforts.

Pillar 3. First the Right Things, then the Things Right

Imagine standing at a crossroads with numerous paths before you, each representing a different route to achieving your goals. The challenge lies in choosing the right path. The key mindset to adopt is one that prioritizes alignment with your objectives—start by identifying what truly resonates with your vision.

Once you've chosen your path, the focus shifts to navigating it with precision and care. This is where the importance of efficiency comes in—ensuring that every step maximizes your resources and efforts, leading you to your destination smoothly and effectively.

Quoting the late Stephen Covey:

> "The most important thing is to **do the right thing**, and the next most important thing is to do the **right thing right**."
> In other words, we start by aiming for **effectiveness**. Then we must strive for **efficiency**.

For years, I've guided my clients through this process, not with abstract theories but with practical, results-oriented solutions. My approach is rooted in leveraging best practices from proven frameworks like design thinking, emotional intelligence, Lean principles, and Agile practices. These frameworks serve as invaluable guides, steering us towards success when applied correctly.

I'm passionate about empowering my clients to move from problem-focused thinking to solution-driven action, helping them achieve their goals effectively and efficiently. Instead of getting stuck on what caused the problem, we explore what might work to overcome it.

Now, let's go beyond theory and dive into the practical application of these ideas. We've already touched on eight powerful frameworks in the previous section—let's explore the first four in greater detail to see how they can be harnessed to achieve tangible results.

Exhibit #14

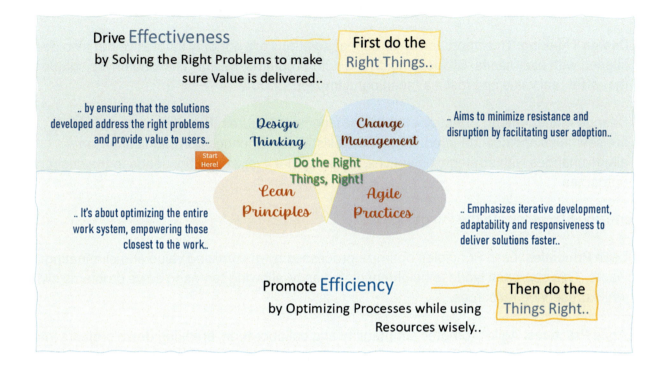

To build on our foundation, let's revisit the key points:

Prioritizing Effectiveness (do the right things):

- **Design Thinking:** This approach ensures that solutions are not only innovative but also deeply aligned with user needs. By focusing on the right problems, Design Thinking drives solutions that offer real value and make a meaningful impact.

- **Change Management:** Effective change management ensures that organizational shifts are seamless and goal oriented. It reduces resistance, enhances communication, and aligns changes with strategic objectives, ensuring that every transition leads to the desired outcomes.

Prioritizing Efficiency (do the things right):

- **Lean Principles:** Lean Principles optimize processes by maximizing value and eliminating waste. This approach leads to heightened efficiency, allowing teams to solve problems swiftly while preserving resources.

- **Agile Practices:** Agile promotes adaptability and collaboration, breaking down projects into manageable tasks and delivering solutions with speed and precision. By embracing change and iterative development, Agile ensures that projects stay on course, even as requirements evolve.

Bottm Line: By first ensuring we're tackling the right challenges and then executing with precision, we set the stage for success. This dual focus on effectiveness and efficiency is the key to not just meeting goals but exceeding them, turning strategies into impactful realities.

Now let's look further and include the second group of frameworks we reviewed afterwards:

Prioritizing Effectiveness (do the right things):

- **Systems Thinking:** This approach promotes a holistic view of interconnected components, helping teams address root causes and achieve sustainable results within the system. It ensures solutions tackle underlying issues rather than just symptoms.

- **Design for Strategy:** This framework guides decision-making to align with strategic goals and drive growth, acting as a compass towards organizational success. It ensures that strategic choices contribute to overarching objectives.

- **The Coaching Mindset:** This philosophy focuses on continuous learning and empowerment. By using the GROW and Solution Focused models, leaders set goals, leverage strengths, and foster a proactive mindset through insightful questioning.

Prioritizing Efficiency (do the things right):

- **Emotional Intelligence (EI):** EI enhances teamwork and decision-making by improving communication, empathy, and self-awareness. Prioritizing EI ensures effective emotion management, maintaining productivity, and achieving goals.

To Sum Up: Integrating these frameworks to the mix promotes both effective decision-making and efficient execution, empowering teams to address root causes, align with strategic goals, and enhance interpersonal dynamics for optimal results.

This is how it all comes together in a single view:

Exhibit #15

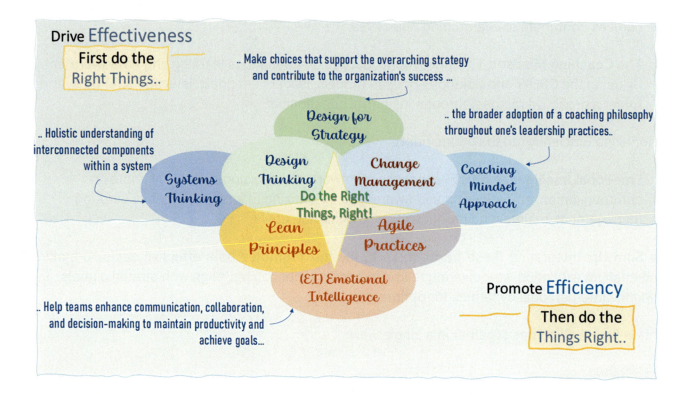

Key Takeaways:

In a nutshell, it's all about finding that sweet spot between effectiveness and efficiency. Here are a couple of key takeaways for you:

1. Choose wisely - Embrace Effectiveness:

Focus on doing the right things first. Choose options that align with your objectives and goals.

Bottm Line: By first ensuring we're tackling the right challenges and then executing with precision, we set the stage for success. This dual focus on effectiveness and efficiency is the key to not just meeting goals but exceeding them, turning strategies into impactful realities.

2. Navigate with ease - Champion Efficiency:

Once you've chosen your path, maximize your resources and efforts to navigate it smoothly and effectively.

3. By applying these principles, you can drive impactful results, align with strategic goals, and enhance team dynamics for sustained success.

Pillar 4. Three Layers of Decision Making

To maximize effectiveness and efficiency, Pillar 3 focused on the importance of making the right choices. Pillar 4 addresses governance by exploring how to make optimal decisions and ensure their successful execution.

For illustration purposes, please refer to Chart #15 below. From left to right, we have a pyramid that illustrates three decision levels—strategic for senior executives, implementation for directors and managers, and operational for subject matter experts and staff—each offering a unique perspective, much like viewing the same situation through different lenses.

At the center, the decision flow highlights the often-challenging transition from planning to execution, which requires careful management of interactions among decision-makers. To the right, the C.H.A.N.G.E.© process introduced earlier serves as a sequential and repeatable framework that supports this transition. This Distributed Decision-Making Blueprint provides a structured approach to governance and transformation, ensuring that decisions are made thoughtfully at every level, and that execution is both effective and aligned with strategic goals.

Embracing this method can equip your organization with a robust framework for governance and transformation, ensuring that decisions are not only well-informed but also executed effectively. This approach aligns strategic intent with operational reality, leading to more coherent, efficient, and successful outcomes.

Let's explore this model further to understand how it can benefit your organization.

Exhibit #16

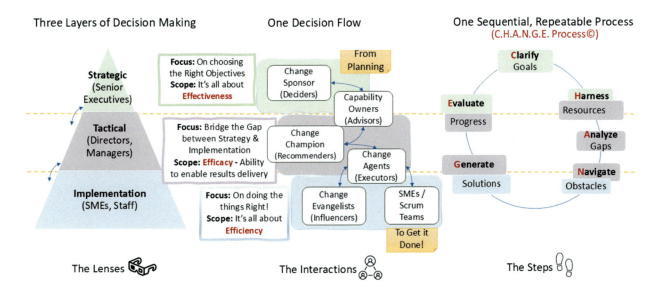

Let's look at each element closely:

For context, let's discuss a hypothetical scenario of how this model could be practically applied within a department of the Government of Canada:

Case Study #1.

Imagine we're part of a team at Environment and Climate Change Canada, working to address climate change and reduce carbon emissions.

1) The Lenses.

Within our department, different decision-makers view challenges through various lenses: senior executives see the strategic big picture, directors and managers focus on tactical implementation, while operational staff handle day-to-day execution. Therefore, we encounter three decision-making layers:

1. **Strategic Decisions:** Senior executives, such as the Minister and top advisors, set the department's overall direction. This might involve forming international agreements, establishing emission targets, or launching major initiatives like the Green Fund.
2. **Tactical Decisions:** Middle managers and department heads take these strategies and determine the best ways to implement them. This includes allocating resources, developing budgets, and coordinating with other departments or stakeholders.
3. **Implementation Decisions:** Front-line staff and supervisors handle the practical aspects of daily operations, such as scheduling climate monitoring, ordering supplies, or responding to public inquiries.

By utilizing these three decision-making layers, our department remains organized and focused, ensuring that strategic goals are effectively translated into actionable steps. This structured approach not only enhances coordination but also drives successful outcomes in our mission to create a more sustainable future for Canada and the planet.

2) The Interactions.

To achieve effective and efficient solutions amidst diverse actors with varying skills, authority, and agendas, it's crucial to adopt a robust decision-making framework. Traditional models like RACI (Responsible, Accountable, Consult, Informed) can often lead to ambiguity, slowed momentum, and frustration due to unclear authority and excessive red tape.

The RACI model may create confusion about decision-makers, stakeholder roles, and approval processes, which can hamper progress and empower reluctance. Meetings often become unproductive, leaving participants questioning their purpose.

Introducing the DARE model.

With all this as background, I recently came across an article from McKinsey. In this, they introduce the DARE model[42] (Deciders, Advisors, Recommenders, Executors) — a different proposition addressing some of RACI's shortcomings. It goes like this: Deciders wield decision-making authority with clarity and purpose. Advisors offer valuable insights without impeding progress. Recommenders meticulously explore options, presenting well-informed recommendations. Lastly, Executors or Execution Stakeholders, which are armed with clear directives, and ensure decisions are smoothly implemented.

If you think about it, it makes total sense. Here's why I think it's better:

1. **Clarity and Focus:** DARE clearly defines roles—Deciders make final decisions, Advisors provide insights, Recommenders explore options, and Executors ensure implementation. This clarity reduces ambiguity and streamlines the decision-making process.
2. **Empowerment:** DARE involves individuals at all levels, allowing broader participation and input. Unlike RACI, which centralizes authority, DARE facilitates meaningful contributions from various stakeholders, enhancing engagement and ownership.
3. **Flexibility:** The model supports a range of roles and contributions, adapting to different decision-making contexts. While Deciders make the final call, Advisors, Recommenders, and Executors each play crucial roles, promoting adaptability and responsiveness.

4. **Action Orientation:** DARE emphasizes timely, actionable decisions. Deciders make clear decisions, while other roles provide necessary information and support, ensuring decisions translate into tangible outcomes.
5. **Implementation Focus: By prioritizing Executors, DARE ensures that decisions are not just made but effectively implemented, driving organizational success and progress.**

In my opinion, while RACI has been a popular choice, DARE offers a more contemporary and adaptable framework. It enhances clarity, empowers participants, offers flexibility, and emphasizes actionable outcomes, making it a superior choice for modern decision-making processes. Adopting DARE can streamline decision-making, improve coordination, and ultimately drive better organizational results.

Before we move any further, let me introduce you to another key concept.

Introducing the Lean Change Management Approach.

I think we all can agree that **any business transformation is at its core a change management challenge.** And as such, tackling it requires a strategic approach. To address this, I'd like to introduce a compelling concept called Lean Change Management, championed by Canadian Jason Little and Portuguese João Gama.

Jason Little's Lean Change Management[43] integrates principles from Lean Startup and Agile methodologies, creating an iterative, adaptive, and feedback-driven process. This approach focuses on incremental change, deeply involving stakeholders and addressing the needs of those impacted by the change, whether they are internal teams or external clients.

João Gama builds on this with the Panoptic Model[44], which emphasizes adaptability and feedback while introducing specific roles such as Change Sponsors, Capability Owners, and Change Champions. These roles ensure that strategic goals translate into tangible results across the organization.

To summarize the key roles:

- **Change Sponsors** are senior leaders responsible for the success of the change initiative, providing strategic direction and resources.
- **Capability Owners** oversee the specific areas undergoing change, ensuring alignment with organizational objectives.
- **Change Champions** promote and support the change, driving engagement and adoption.
- **Change Agents** execute the change on the ground, adjusting plans as needed based on feedback.
- **Change Evangelists** build grassroots support, fostering a positive narrative around the change.
- **Scrum Teams & SMEs** manage projects using the Scrum methodology, driving continuous improvement.

These roles work together to ensure that change initiatives are executed smoothly, aligning with the organization's goals while fostering resilience and engagement among employees.

Now, if we merge this approach with the DARE model, we create a powerful synergy (depicted at the center of Exhibit #15 as "One Decision Flow"):

- **Change Sponsors** (Deciders) work strategically with **Capability Owners** (Advisors),
- **Capability Owners** collaborate with **Change Champions** (Recommenders) at the tactical level,
- **Change Champions** work with **Change Agents** (Executors) to implement change, supported by **Change Evangelists** who positively influence their peers.

By integrating these models, you create a robust framework that aligns strategic intent with operational execution, ensuring coherence and coordination across all levels of the organization. This approach not only addresses the complexities of change management but also enhances decision-making and implementation, leading to more successful outcomes.

To wrap-up this section, let's put all the pieces of Exhibit #15 together and explore how the Distributed Decision-Making Blueprint can effectively address the complexities of our case study, ensuring seamless and repeatable decision-making processes across multiple layers of the organization. This is how it would work:

- **Deciders (Strategic Layer):**

    - **Who:** Senior Executives, including the Minister and top advisors.
    - **Role:** Deciders set the strategic direction, focusing on high-level objectives like forming international agreements or establishing emission targets. In Exhibit #15, they are personified by the **"Change Sponsor"** who ensures that decisions align with overarching goals, driving the policy direction.
    - **Focus:** Choosing the **Right Objectives**
    - **Scope:** It's all about **Effectiveness**
    - C.H.A.N.G.E. Process© Alignment:
    Clarify Goals: Deciders are responsible for setting clear, strategic objectives that guide the department's efforts, ensuring alignment with broader policies and strategies.

- **Advisors (Tactical Layer):**

    - **Who:** Experts, directors, and managers.
    - **Role:** Advisors provide insights and guidance, bridging the gap between strategy and implementation. They are aligned with the **"Capability Owners"**, focusing on the effectiveness of strategies by ensuring they are feasible and actionable within the department.
    - **Focus:** Bridge the Gap between Strategy & Implementation
    - **Scope: Efficacy** - Ability to **enable results delivery**
    - C.H.A.N.G.E. Process© Alignment:
    Harness Resources: Advisors ensure that all resources—financial, human, and technical—are identified and allocated effectively, supporting the strategic goals set by Deciders.
    Generate Solutions: Advisors collaborate with Recommenders to generate and refine practical, effective solutions that align with departmental goals.

- **Recommenders (Tactical Layer):**

    - **Who:** Middle Managers, Team Leads.

- **Role:** Recommenders evaluate options and present well-rounded recommendations. This role is embodied by "**Change Champions**" who advocate for the best course of action, ensuring decisions are well-informed and actionable.
- **Focus:** Bridge the Gap between Strategy & Implementation
- **Scope: Efficacy** - Ability to **enable results delivery**
- C.H.A.N.G.E. Process© Alignment:
  Analyze Gaps: Recommenders evaluate existing conditions, identify gaps, and present solutions that align with strategic objectives, ensuring readiness for implementation.
  Generate Solutions: Recommenders collaborate with Advisors to develop actionable solutions that meet the department's needs.

- **Executors (Implementation Layer):**

  - **Who:** Operational Staff, Front-line Supervisors.
  - **Role:** Executors are responsible for the day-to-day implementation of the policy, as indicated by the "**Change Agents**" in said exhibit. They focus on translating decisions into practical actions, ensuring that the strategic goals set by Deciders are achieved through effective execution.
  - **Focus: Doing the things Right!**
  - **Scope:** It's all about **Efficiency**
  - C.H.A.N.G.E. Process© Alignment:
    Navigate Obstacles: Executors manage and overcome challenges during execution, ensuring that strategic objectives are met on time and within scope.
    Evaluate Progress: Executors provide ground-level feedback to Deciders and Recommenders, allowing for adjustments and course corrections as necessary.

Bottom line:

The Distributed Decision-Making Blueprint, when integrated with the DARE model and the C.H.A.N.G.E.© process, offers a structured and repeatable approach to governance that aligns decision-making across strategic, tactical, and operational levels. This comprehensive framework not only clarifies roles and responsibilities but also ensures that decisions flow seamlessly from strategy to execution, enhancing coordination, empowering stakeholders, and driving effective implementation.

By adopting this methodology, public organizations like Environment and Climate Change Canada in our example can achieve their mission with greater efficiency and impact, ultimately contributing to a more sustainable future.

Key Takeaways

1. **Clarity in Roles:** The DARE model provides clear definitions of decision-making roles, ensuring that each layer of governance is aligned and empowered to contribute effectively.
2. **Seamless Decision Flow:** The integration of the DARE model with the C.H.A.N.G.E.© process creates a smooth transition from strategic planning to operational execution, reducing friction and enhancing coordination.
3. **Empowerment Across Levels:** By involving Advisors, Recommenders, and Executors, the framework fosters broader participation, ensuring that all voices are heard and valued in the decision-making process.
4. **Action-Oriented Decisions:** The model emphasizes actionable decisions, ensuring that strategic goals are translated into practical, on-the-ground outcomes.
5. **Improved Implementation:** With a focus on execution, the framework ensures that decisions are not only made but also implemented effectively, driving successful transformation and achieving organizational objectives.

3) The Steps.

Consulting Case Study #4. Part 1: Transformation in the Federal Health Sector.

To illustrate the practical application of my model, I'll provide an example from a past consulting engagement. While I'm unable to share specific client details due to confidentiality agreements, this case involves a transformation initiative within a federal health agency's Corporate Management Directorate. This example will demonstrate how the model was applied to drive significant improvements in their organizational processes.

The directorate faced significant challenges in modernizing its business administration functions amidst operational complexities. This example highlights how the C.H.A.N.G.E. Framework for Doing the Right Things Right© was employed to drive a successful transformation, streamline service delivery, and enhance overall efficiency.

Before my intervention:

The directorate was grappling with a range of critical challenges that impeded its ability to operate efficiently, collaborate effectively, and streamline its administrative functions. The absence of a unified strategic vision for business operations resulted in fragmented efforts and inefficiencies. Outdated systems and resistance to change further exacerbated these issues, leading to delays, increased costs, and a diminished capacity to adapt to the agency's evolving needs. Ineffective resource allocation and a lack of support for transformative initiatives hindered progress and innovation.

Communication channels were poor, leading to misunderstandings and a lack of buy-in from employees. This resistance stalled the adoption of new processes. The directorate operated in silos with limited collaboration, causing duplicated efforts and missed opportunities for optimization. Additionally, the organizational culture was misaligned with the transformation goals, causing employee disconnection and skepticism that impeded success.

Moreover, there was a lack of real-time operational visibility and inadequate feedback mechanisms, which led to poor decision-making and slow responses to emerging challenges. The directorate struggled to innovate and adapt to market and technological changes, resulting in missed opportunities and reduced effectiveness.

Situation After Intervention:

After applying the C.H.A.N.G.E. Framework for Doing the Right Things Right©, the directorate saw significant improvements. Previously, we covered the 3 steps and 4 pillars. The following visual offers a comprehensive overview of the step-by-step process for better understanding.

Exhibit #17

Step #1: Defining the Mission Possible (The What):

The intervention began by asking key questions to define the mission:

- **What do you want to achieve?**

The directorate sought to establish a clear, cohesive strategic direction for its business operations, leading to unified efforts across units and streamlined processes. This aimed to eliminate redundancies and enhance coordination and efficiency.

- **What do you want to avoid?**

The directorate wanted to avoid fragmentation, inefficiencies, and delays that resulted from a lack of strategic direction.

- **What's your Value Proposition?**

Through collaborative discussions, the directorate articulated its value propositions:

- "Unify our administrative operations with a clear strategic direction, eliminating redundancies and streamlining processes for maximum efficiency."
- "Achieve seamless coordination and improved efficiency across our organization by establishing a cohesive strategic vision for business operations."

By aligning all efforts with unified strategic goals, redundancies were reduced, and progress toward common objectives was accelerated.

Step #2: Foreseeing a Clear Vision of the Finish Line (The Why):

- **Why was it needed?**

A strategic vision was set to unify the directorate's efforts, enhancing operational efficiency, reducing delays and costs, and improving service reliability.

- **Why was it a game changer?**

This transformation addressed existing challenges and fostered operational effectiveness, benefiting both the agency and its employees. By streamlining operations and enhancing synergy, the directorate achieved smoother and more cost-effective service delivery.

Step #3: Applying the C.H.A.N.G.E.© Framework (How can we make this happen?):

1. **Clarified Goals:**
   A comprehensive assessment of the directorate's business processes was conducted. Challenges related to inefficiencies and outdated technologies were identified, and clear transformation goals were set to improve efficiency, reduce costs, and enhance agility.

2. **Harnessed Resources:**
   Support was secured from senior executives and stakeholders, and resources were mobilized using Agile and Lean techniques. A cross-functional team was assembled to provide diverse expertise and support.

3. **Analyzed Gaps:**
   A gap analysis was performed to compare current operations with desired outcomes, identifying discrepancies and their impact on achieving transformation goals.

4. **Navigated Obstacles:**
   Lean Startup principles were used to address challenges through iterative experimentation, and practical strategies were developed for implementation, considering potential obstacles.

5. **Generated Solutions:**
   Innovative solutions were developed through brainstorming and design thinking sessions, and new technologies were implemented to optimize processes.

6. **Evaluated Progress:**
   Implementing OKRs (Objectives and Key Results), a framework for setting and tracking objectives and key results, enabled ongoing evaluation and adjustment. This fostered a culture of continuous improvement by encouraging regular feedback and accountability.

Leveraging the Four Pillars:

- **Pillar #1: Adopted New Mindsets**
  The focus shifted from problems to opportunities, emphasizing the importance of seeing the bigger picture, embracing adaptability, using resources efficiently, and engaging in critical thinking. Key questions were asked:
    - "What Problem are we trying to solve?"
    - "What Opportunity are we trying to seize?"

The directorate responded with insights such as:
  - "Our current mindset might be hindering our ability to embrace agile methodologies and adapt quickly to changing circumstances."
  - "Our focus on short-term goals might be preventing us from investing in long-term growth opportunities."
  - "Our focus on maintaining the status quo might be preventing us from exploring disruptive innovations that could transform our operations."

- **Pillar #2: Applied Best Practices from Proven Frameworks**
  The success of the transformation was underpinned by a combination of well-established frameworks, tailored to the unique needs of the directorate. Systems Thinking was used to understand complex interactions, Agile for iterative development, Lean Principles for optimizing resources, and Design for Strategy for decision-making:

Systems Thinking:

This approach was crucial in understanding and addressing the complex interactions within the directorate. By viewing the organization as an interconnected system, it became possible to identify root causes of inefficiencies and implement holistic solutions that addressed the broader impact on the agency's operations.

Agile Methodology:

Agile practices were employed to manage the transformation in an iterative and flexible manner. This allowed for rapid adjustments based on feedback and ensured that the solutions remained relevant and effective throughout the transformation process. The directorate benefited from increased responsiveness and adaptability, leading to more efficient project management and timely delivery of outcomes.

Lean Principles:

Lean methodologies were applied to optimize resource utilization, eliminate waste, and streamline processes. This approach led to a more efficient allocation of resources, reducing costs and enhancing the overall effectiveness of the directorate's operations.

Design for Strategy:

This framework was used to guide critical decision-making, ensuring that strategic choices were aligned with the overarching goals of the transformation. By integrating strategic design into the decision-making process, the directorate was able to make informed, forward-thinking choices that supported long-term success.

- **Pillar #3: Did the Right Things Right**
Ensuring that the directorate not only did the right things but did them right was central to the transformation's success. Strategic goals were defined, transformation opportunities were identified, and change was managed effectively using proven models. Agile practices, Lean principles, and Emotional Intelligence were applied to ensure efficiency and enhanced collaboration:

Strategic Goal Definition:

Clear, strategic goals were established at the outset, providing a roadmap for the transformation. These goals were designed to be achievable, measurable, and aligned with the directorate's mission, ensuring that all efforts were directed toward meaningful outcomes.

Opportunity Identification:

Throughout the transformation, continuous efforts were made to identify and capitalize on opportunities for improvement. This proactive approach allowed the directorate to stay ahead of potential challenges and leverage emerging trends to its advantage.

Effective Change Management:

The transformation was managed using a combination of Agile practices, Lean principles, and Emotional Intelligence. This multifaceted approach ensured that changes were implemented smoothly, with minimal disruption to operations, and that employees were engaged and supportive throughout the process. Emotional Intelligence played a key role in addressing resistance to change, fostering a positive cu

- **Pillar #4: Layered Decision Making for successful outcomes.**
The transformation was anchored in a structured decision-making framework across three layers:

Deciders:

The top layer consisted of senior executives who set the strategic objectives for the transformation. Their role was to ensure that the transformation aligned with the agency's mission and long-term vision. They provided the necessary support and resources, making high-level decisions that guided the overall direction of the transformation.

Advisors:

The middle layer included advisors who played a crucial role in bridging strategy and implementation. They were responsible for translating strategic goals into actionable plans, providing guidance and expertise to ensure that the transformation was executed effectively. Advisors also facilitated communication between the deciders and executors, ensuring alignment and coherence across all levels of the directorate.

Executors:

The bottom layer consisted of those responsible for carrying out the day-to-day actions required to implement the transformation. Executors were empowered to make operational decisions within the framework provided by the advisors and deciders, ensuring that the transformation was implemented efficiently and effectively. Their role was to execute the plans with precision, monitor progress, and make necessary adjustments to achieve the desired outcomes.

Outcome:

This layered approach ensured alignment from strategy to execution, enhancing coordination, empowering stakeholders, and driving effective outcomes. By clearly defining roles and responsibilities across these layers, the directorate was able to maintain focus, ensure accountability, and achieve a successful transformation.

Bottom Line:

Applying the C.H.A.N.G.E. Framework for Doing the Right Things Right©, led to a significant transformation of the directorate. It provided a clear strategic direction, streamlined operations, and fostered innovation, addressing operational challenges and enhancing efficiency and responsiveness. By defining clear goals, harnessing resources effectively, and overcoming obstacles through innovative solutions, the organization drove meaningful change and optimized outcomes.

This structured approach not only addressed existing issues but also positioned the directorate for sustainable success, aligning strategic vision with operational execution and achieving lasting impact.

Part Four. Bringing It All Together.

"Skills are never enough. Knowledge must be accompanied by action."
— Daniel Kahneman

Primary Outcomes.

Having explored the step-by-step application of the C.H.A.N.G.E. Framework for Doing the Right Things Right©, it's now time to delve into the tangible outcomes that result from its implementation. The real power of this framework lies in its ability to deliver three critical results: a strategic Roadmap, a detailed Blueprint, and a tangible Minimum Viable Product, Service, or Change (MVP/MVS/MVC). These outcomes are not just abstract concepts but concrete deliverables that can guide your organization toward successful and sustainable transformation. Let's explore what each of these outcomes entails and how they can be leveraged to drive meaningful change.

Here's how it all fits together:

1. The Roadmap: Strategic Guidance For Transformation

The Roadmap serves as the strategic guide for your transformation journey. It outlines the high-level vision, goals, and key milestones that your organization aims to achieve over a specified period. This strategic tool provides clear direction, aligning all stakeholders on the path to success. It helps prioritize initiatives, allocate resources efficiently, and set realistic timelines, ensuring that every step taken is purposeful and aligned with broader objectives.

By defining a Roadmap, leaders foster a shared understanding and commitment across the organization, setting the stage for cohesive and coordinated efforts.

How could this be illustrated visually?

- Visual Concept: A timeline infographic.

- Description: Display a horizontal timeline with key milestones marked along it. Include icons or symbols representing each milestone, such as a calendar icon for dates, a gear icon for the digital platform rollout, and a book icon for training programs. Example:

Exhibit #18

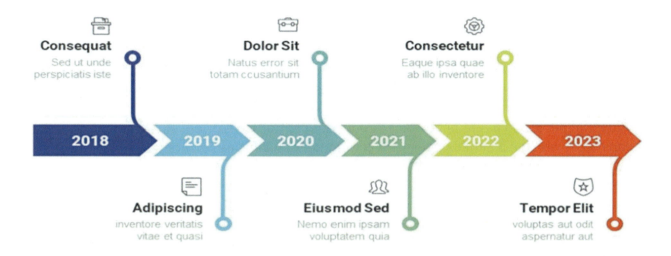

2. The Blueprint: Translating Vision into Action

The Blueprint translates the strategic vision into a detailed tactical plan. It acts as the architectural design of your transformation, providing a comprehensive layout of the processes, systems, and structures necessary to achieve defined goals. This plan includes specifications, standards, and guidelines required to build and implement transformation initiatives. By creating a Blueprint, leaders can visualize the end state, identify potential challenges, and devise solutions proactively.

The Blueprint serves as a reference point throughout the transformation, ensuring that all actions are consistent with the planned design and contribute to the desired outcomes.

How can this be depicted visually?

- Visual: A flowchart or architectural diagram.

- Description: Create a detailed schematic of the new digital portal and service delivery model. Include boxes or nodes for each major component, such as technological infrastructure, data migration, and integration points. Connect these components with arrows to show how they interact. Add callouts or side notes to specify roles, responsibilities, and workflow changes.

- Example:

Exhibit #19

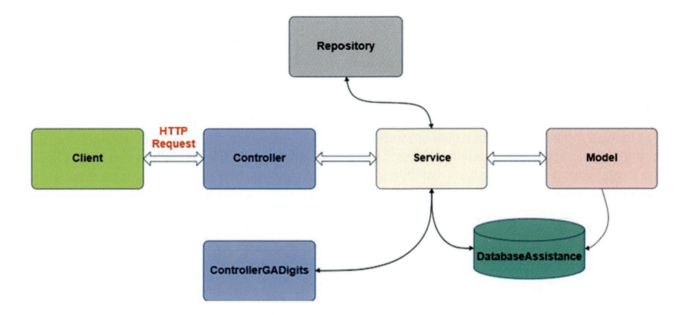

An MVP, MVS, and MVC: Tangible Implementation with Iterative Value

The Minimum Viable Product (MVP), Minimum Viable Service (MVS), and Minimum Viable Change (MVC) represents the implementation layer of your transformation efforts, offering the first tangible outcome that delivers value while meeting essential requirements. Depending on the nature of your transformation, you may need just one of these, a pair, or a combination of all three:

3. Minimum Viable Product (MVP):

This is the simplest version of a new product that can be released to the market. It includes only the core features necessary to satisfy early adopters and gather feedback. Developing an MVP allows you to test your product's viability, validate assumptions, and make necessary adjustments before investing in full-scale production.

This approach helps you avoid costly mistakes and ensures that the final product is closely aligned with user needs and market demands.

Use case:

Imagine your organization is developing a new health tracking mobile app. The MVP would be the initial version of this app, which includes only the core features such as step counting, basic heart rate monitoring, and a simple user interface. This version is released to a small group of users to gather feedback.

The purpose of the MVP is to validate the concept, test user engagement, and identify any critical issues before investing in a full-featured product. It's the first tangible product output that aligns with the transformation goals while minimizing risk

How can this be represented visually?

- Visual Concept: Screenshot or wireframe of the MVP interface.
- Description: Provide a mockup or wireframe of the basic version of the digital portal, highlighting the essential functions like the unified login system and core administrative services. Annotate the MVP with feedback points where user interactions are highlighted and use callout bubbles to show areas for improvement based on initial feedback.
- Example:

Exhibit #20

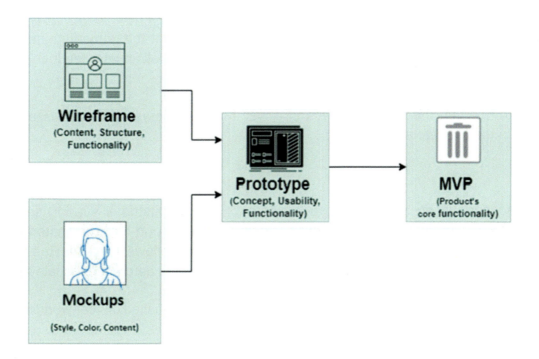

4. Minimum Viable Service (MVS):

Like an MVP, an MVS focuses on delivering the core elements of a new service. It allows you to introduce a service offering with just enough functionality to meet the immediate needs of your users. By rolling out an MVS, you can quickly demonstrate value, collect user feedback, and refine the service iteratively.

This helps ensure that the service evolves in a way that best serves your clients and remains competitive in the marketplace.

Use case:

Consider a scenario where your organization wants to improve customer support services. The MVS could be a pilot program that introduces a new customer support team dedicated to handling a limited set of common issues. This small-scale implementation allows you to test the new service approach, gather feedback from customers, and refine the service before a full-scale rollout.

The MVS helps in demonstrating early value, improving the service based on real-world interactions, and ensuring the service model is effective before expanding.

What is the best way to visualize this?

- Visual Concept: Pilot phase diagram or process flowchart.

- Description: Visualize the pilot phase with a process flowchart that outlines the journey from understanding customer problems to delivering a refined solution. Depict stages like problem identification, solution development, and implementation, using distinct colors or shapes to differentiate the different business units.

- Example:

Exhibit #21

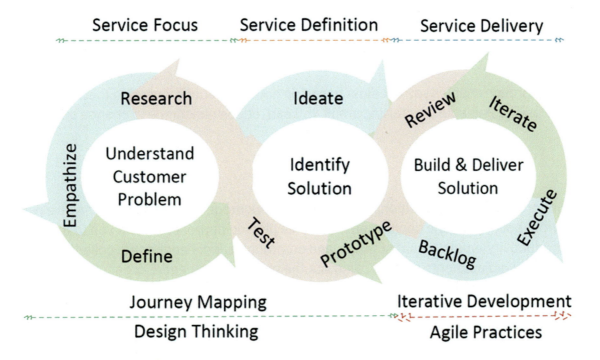

5. Minimum Viable Change (MVC):

When the transformation involves internal processes or organizational shifts, an MVC is key. It represents the smallest set of changes that can be implemented to start delivering measurable improvements. Focusing on small, manageable changes can help you avoid overwhelming your team.

This iterative approach enables you to adjust based on actual feedback, ensuring that the change is both effective and sustainable. By starting small, you can reduce resistance to change and increase buy-in.

Use case:

Suppose your organization is transitioning to a remote work model. The MVC could involve piloting the remote work policy with one department first. This phased approach allows you to monitor the impact on productivity, employee satisfaction, and communication. Feedback is collected regularly to make necessary adjustments before rolling out the change to the entire organization.

The MVC focuses on achieving early wins and ensuring that the change is sustainable and effective before broader implementation.

What visual approach can be used to illustrate this?

- Visual Concept: Before-and-after process comparison chart.

- Description: Create a side-by-side comparison chart showing the process before and after the initial realignment. Use visuals like arrows or flow diagrams to depict how a specific process was streamlined. Highlight key improvements, such as reduced confusion and enhanced tracking, with specific metrics or icons. Example:

Exhibit #22

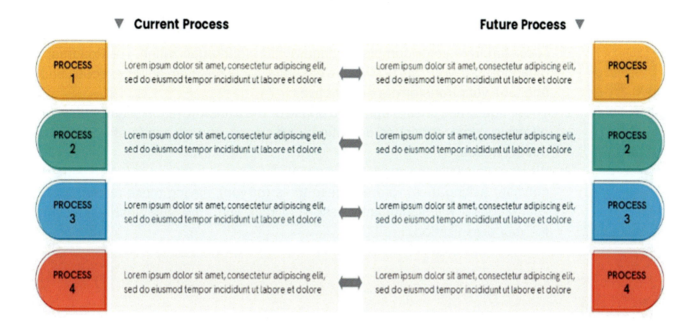

These examples illustrate how the MVP, MVS, and MVC are practical, iterative tools that align with the C.H.A.N.G.E. Framework to drive successful, sustainable transformation. Each one offers a practical way to secure quick wins, validate strategies, and mitigate risks. Whether you need one, two, or all three, they are crucial tools for accelerating the transformation process and ensuring that your initiatives lead to successful, long-term outcomes.

Takeaways:

1. For leaders or those stepping into a transformation role, the C.H.A.N.G.E. Framework for Doing the Right Things Right© offers a structured pathway to successfully manage complex changes within your organization. The Roadmap, Blueprint, and MVP/MVS/MVC are essential tools that help guide, execute, and fine-tune your transformation initiatives.
2. These outcomes ensure that each phase of the transformation aligns with your strategic goals, enhances operational efficiency, and responds effectively to market needs.
3. Whether you have the support of a specialized consultant or not (and if you do, consider asking them to draft these tools for you), having these resources at your disposal will significantly ease your task and drive sustainable success for your organization.

Driving Tangible Outcomes: Leveraging the C.H.A.N.G.E. Framework
Consulting Case Study #4. Part 2: the Roadmap, Blueprint, and MVP/MVS/MVC.

Having detailed the C.H.A.N.G.E. Framework for Doing the Right Things Right©, we now focus on the tangible outcomes that it generates: the Roadmap, Blueprint, and MVP/MVS/MVC. This section revisits Consulting Case Study #4 to reveal how the elements were applied to guide, execute, and refine their transformation process. The key point is that these are not just theoretical concepts but essential tools that drove our transformation to success.

Please note that due to confidentiality constraints, specific details cannot be disclosed. We will explore each element in detail, drawing from the case study to demonstrate their practical application. Additionally, I will offer suggestions on how to visualize these concepts effectively, ensuring a clear and engaging representation of their role in the transformation process.

1. **Roadmap: Strategic Guide for Transformation**

In the transformation of the Corporate Management Directorate (CMD), the Roadmap served as the strategic guide, outlining the long-term vision to centralize and streamline business services under a unified service delivery model. It detailed the key milestones over a three-year period, including the consolidation of departmental services, the rollout of a new digital platform, and the retraining of staff to support the new operational processes.

The Roadmap provided clarity on the sequence of initiatives, ensuring that each phase was built on top of the previous one and aligned with the overall strategic objectives of improving service efficiency and client satisfaction.

2. **Blueprint: Detailed Tactical Plan**

The Blueprint translated the strategic vision of the Directorate's transformation into a comprehensive tactical plan. It included detailed schematics of the new centralized digital portal, specifying the technological infrastructure required, data migration processes, and the integration points with existing systems.

The Blueprint also outlined the roles and responsibilities of staff, the workflow changes needed to support the new service delivery model, and the training programs designed to equip employees with the necessary skills. This document became the reference point for all stakeholders, ensuring that every implementation step was aligned with the designed end-state and that potential challenges were proactively addressed.

3. Minimum Viable Product (MVP): Initial Digital Platform

As part of the transformation, the initial Minimum Viable Product (MVP) was a basic version of the centralized digital portal. This MVP included only the most critical functions—such as a unified login system and access to core administrative services like HR requests and financial processing.

By releasing this MVP early in the process, the Directorate was able to gather feedback from a small group of end-users, validate the user interface design, and identify any immediate issues that needed correction. This allowed for quick adjustments before the full-scale deployment of the portal, ensuring that the final product met the needs of all users across the agency.

4. Minimum Viable Service (MVS): Pilot of New Service Delivery Model

An MVS was created by piloting the new centralized service delivery model within one department of the Directorate. This pilot included the reorganization of administrative functions into a single point of contact for staff, the implementation of the new service protocols, and the training of a select group of employees on the new processes.

The pilot aimed to test the efficiency and responsiveness of the new model in a controlled environment, allowing the leadership to collect data, measure outcomes, and make informed decisions before rolling out the service model to the entire Directorate. The success of this MVS provided proof of concept, demonstrating the benefits of the new model and building momentum for broader implementation.

5. Minimum Viable Change (MVC): Initial Process Realignment

The MVC involved implementing the smallest set of process changes to begin improving efficiency within the Directorate. One such change was the realignment of the business services intake process, where all incoming requests were funneled through a single digital channel instead of multiple email addresses. This change was minimal yet impactful, as it reduced confusion, streamlined request tracking, and provided immediate data on service bottlenecks.

The MVC allowed the Directorate to start realizing the benefits of the transformation without overwhelming the organization with too many changes at once, paving the way for more comprehensive process improvements down the line.

These examples illustrate how each outcome of the C.H.A.N.G.E. Framework plays a crucial role in driving a successful transformation within a complex organization like the CMD. They provide a structured approach to not only plan and design the transformation but also to implement and refine it in a way that maximizes value and minimizes risk. Whether your organization is developing new systems, enhancing service delivery, or implementing significant change, these tools will equip you to navigate complexities effectively.

Connecting the Dots: Turning Knowledge into Action

You now have the insights I've developed over two decades, tested in real-world scenarios with clients. But knowing what to do is just the start—true transformation happens through implementation.

Consider the ADKAR model, which shows that awareness alone isn't enough for effective change. Genuine progress requires a desire to change, which drives the acquisition of knowledge and skills. This idea is central to successfully applying The C.H.A.N.G.E. Framework for Doing the Right Things Right©.

With that in mind, you will remember that in Part 3, we explored how the GROWth Solution Mindset Coaching© begins with defining a clear vision and assessing the current state to identify strengths and areas for improvement. From there, it sets motivating goals and creates actionable, time-bound plans, all while fostering ongoing feedback and adjustments.

This approach itself enables individuals to become effective internal coaches regardless of their background by applying these principles in practical situations.

However, I am aware that for some folks it may be quite challenging, or they may not have the time available to coach people on top of their managerial responsibilities. Furthermore, to fully realize the potential of this model, practical application and adaptation are essential, which could make it even more challenging for those without previous coaching experience.

That's why I developed SKILLSHIFT Coaching©—a tailored approach designed to guide you in implementing, customizing, and scaling these strategies for sustained success.

Through SKILLSHIFT Coaching©, I integrate the GROWth Solution Mindset with the C.H.A.N.G.E. Framework for Doing the Right Things Right© to achieve tangible results. In the next section, I'll show you how SKILLSHIFT Coaching© has achieved exceptional results for clients and how it can transform your organization.

Consulting Case Study #4. Part 3: the GROWth Solution Mindset Coaching©.

To illustrate the effectiveness of my coaching method, let's take up once again the case of our Federal Health Sector client. Together with my clients, we customized the 6-step GROWth Solution Mindset and integrated it with the C.H.A.N.G.E. Framework to address their specific challenges, ensuring a focused and adaptable transformation.

Here's how the 6-step sequence was implemented within a 20-week timeline:

Weeks 1-2: **Step 1 - Define the "Winning Aspiration" (Vision)**

- **C.H.A.N.G.E. Framework Alignment**: Phase in line with Step 1 of **C.H.A.N.G.E. – the WHAT**. The mission was clearly defined, ensuring the vision for the administrative directorate focused on modernizing business processes, streamlining operations, and collaboration.
- **Activities:** Conducted stakeholder workshops to articulate vision, analyze current state.
- **Deliverables:** Vision Statement, Current State Report, Desired Future Overview.

- **Vision:** Created a unified, efficient, and agile administrative directorate that supported the agency's mission with modernized business processes, streamlined operations, and collaborative team efforts.
- **Current State:** Fragmented efforts, outdated systems, resistance to change.
- **Desired Future:** Seamless coordination, strategic direction, high-performance operations.

Weeks 3-4: **Step 2 - Assess the Current Reality**

- **C.H.A.N.G.E. Framework Alignment**: This connected to Step 2 – **the WHY**.
Strengths and weaknesses were assessed, and stakeholder feedback helped clarify the purpose and human impact of the transformation, highlighting the need for collaboration.

- **Activities:** Strengths and weaknesses assessment, established support network, gathered feedback.
- **Deliverables:** Current Reality Assessment Report, Support Network Plan.
    - **Strengths:** A motivated leadership team and a desire for change within certain groups.
    - **Areas for Improvement:** Inefficient communication, lack of collaboration, siloed operations, outdated technology, and limited strategic direction.
    - **upport Network:** Engaged key stakeholders across departments to build buy-in and ensure the leadership team was aligned.

Weeks 5-7: **Step 3 - Explore Options**

- **C.H.A.N.G.E. Framework Alignment**: This phase reflected Step 3 – **the HOW**.
Goals were clarified, resources were harnessed, and gaps were analyzed through workshops and strategy evaluations. Proven frameworks like Design Thinking and Lean methodologies were used, aligning with the C.H.A.N.G.E. Framework's pillar of leveraging best practices.

- **Activities:** Facilitated strategy workshops, evaluated potential pathways, selected best options.
- **Deliverables:** Options Analysis Report, Recommended Pathways Document.

Pathways for Change:

1. Implemented an **agile project management** structure to modernize processes incrementally.
2. Used **design thinking workshops** to identify pain points and innovate solutions for collaboration.
3. **Applied Lean methodologies** to eliminate redundancies and optimize resource allocation.

Weeks 8-9: **Step 4 - Set Inspirational Goals**

- **C.H.A.N.G.E. Framework Alignment**: This phase focused on solution generation, integral to **the HOW,** by setting inspirational goals to unify and motivate the team. The clear goal setting echoed the framework's pillar of adopting new mindsets and forward-thinking.
- **Activities:** Defined and refined Inspirational Goals, aligned with vision and current reality.
- **Deliverables:** Inspirational Goals and Alignment Report.

Goals:
- **Unify operations** by creating cross-functional teams that collaborate on shared objectives.
- **Modernize administrative functions** through technology adoption and agile practices.
- **Increase staff engagement** by improving communication and alignment with the agency's mission.

Weeks 10-12: **Step 5 - Develop SMART Action Plans**

- **C.H.A.N.G.E. Framework Alignment:** This step further developed **the HOW** by creating specific, time-bound action plans that prioritized both effectiveness and efficiency, key takeaways from the C.H.A.N.G.E. Framework.
- **Activities:** Created detailed action plans, defined milestones and deadlines, assigned responsibilities.
- **Deliverables:** SMART Action Plans, Milestones and Deadlines Schedule.

Action Steps:

1. Conducted a **comprehensive assessment** of current processes and systems.
2. Organized **cross-departmental workshops** to align on strategic vision and collaboration.
3. Designed a **phased technology upgrade plan** that addresses critical areas first.
4. Set **clear milestones and deliverables** for each phase of the transformation.

Weeks 13-20: **Step 6 - Implement, Monitor, and Adapt**

- **C.H.A.N.G.E. Framework Alignment**: This phase implemented and monitored the transformation process, integrating continuous feedback and adaptability, **key aspects of the HOW** in the C.H.A.N.G.E. Framework. Progress was monitored through OKRs (Objectives and Key Results), ensuring a balanced focus on effectiveness and efficiency.
- **Activities:** Executed action plans, monitored progress, gathered feedback, adapted strategies as needed.
- **Deliverables:** Implementation Progress Reports, Feedback Summaries, Adapted Strategies Plan.
  - **Execution:** Empowered teams with the responsibility to execute action plans, with frequent check-ins to assess progress.
  - **Monitoring:** Used OKRs to track progress against objectives and key results. Incorporated feedback loops to continuously adapt and refine strategies.
  - **Adaptation:** Encouraged responsiveness to evolving challenges and market conditions by fostering a mindset of continuous improvement.

To conclude this section, I can proudly tell you that my coaching framework significantly enhanced leadership and team culture within the Directorate by fostering resilience and collaboration. By emphasizing transparency, communication, and shared success, it transformed skepticism and resistance into robust support. This approach not only promoted agility but also empowered teams to embrace ownership of the transformation journey, leading to sustainable growth.

With SKILLSHIFT Coaching©, the directorate successfully evolved from fragmented efforts to a unified, high-performing operation.

Takeaways:

1. **The C.H.A.N.G.E. Framework for Doing the Right Things Right© is the Structure**—A systematic approach to transformation that integrates best practices from proven frameworks, ensuring focus on effective actions and efficient execution.
2. **The GROWth Solution Mindset© is the Strategy**—A strategic approach focused on leveraging strengths and resources to build solutions, fostering a growth-oriented, adaptable environment rather than dwelling on root cause of problems.
3. **SKILLSHIFT Coaching© is the Delivery Metho**d—A practical application of the GROWth Solution Mindset and the C.H.A.N.G.E. Framework for Doing the Right Things Right, tailored to address specific client challenges and drive measurable, impactful outcomes.

Consulting Case Study #5.
Addressing System Challenges through Design Thinking

In this section, I'll walk you through a real-world example of how I applied Design Thinking to help a key federal government client in the external sector address challenges within two complex systems. While I must omit specific details, the focus was on guiding their Operations and Digital Innovation Division through critical changes and innovations, particularly in outreach, stakeholder management, and resolving system issues outlined in their annual Operations Plan.

The Challenge:

The client's mission-critical systems required an extensive outreach initiative to both internal and external stakeholders. This included collecting, identifying, and analyzing system challenges, and ultimately proposing viable solutions. My role was not only to facilitate this process but also to ensure that the solutions were user-centered, realistic, and sustainable.

My Approach:

I applied the Design Thinking Double Diamond methodology—an integral part of my signature framework. As explained earlier in part 3, Design Thinking is a structured approach to problem-solving that centers on understanding user needs, exploring a variety of solutions, and iterating to find the best fit. The process is visually represented as two diamond shapes: one for discovering and defining the problem, and the other for finding and refining the solution.

For simplicity, let's revisit again Exhibit #5 seen in Part 3:

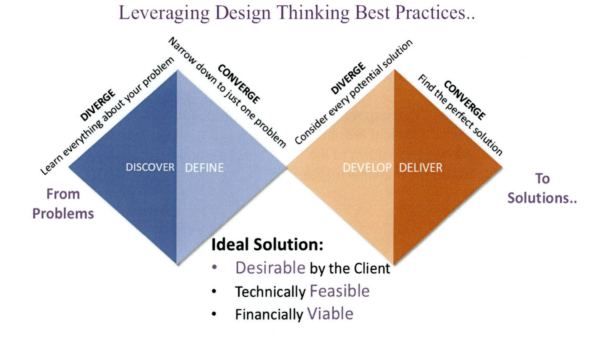

*Altered version of the original Double Diamond model by the British Design Council

Here's how my intervention played out:

Phase 1: Discovery and Definition

- Divergence: We kicked things off by identifying and prioritizing key stakeholders, based on their influence and interest. From there, I led outreach activities—surveys, interviews, and feedback sessions—designed to gather insights into the system's existing issues and challenges.

- Convergence: Once we had all the feedback, I dove into analyzing the data to pinpoint the core system challenges. This step was crucial in making sure we were tackling the right problems, homing in on the issues that mattered most to the client's operations.

Phase 2: Development and Refinement

- Divergence: With the problems clearly defined, I facilitated a series of workshops and brainstorming sessions where we explored a wide range of potential solutions. These collaborative sessions encouraged fresh thinking and helped us creatively address the system challenges.

- Convergence: After brainstorming, we evaluated each proposed solution using three key criteria: desirability for the client, technical feasibility, and financial viability. Through close collaboration with stakeholders, we narrowed down to the most practical and promising solutions that aligned with the client's needs and operational realities.

Deliverables and Timeline:

The entire project spanned 12 weeks, during which I delivered:

1. Outreach Strategy/Plan: By the end of the first month, I developed a clear strategy, detailing the methods, communication channels, and outreach materials to engage stakeholders.
2. Surveys/Questionnaires: I designed and distributed tools to gather essential feedback from both internal and external clients.
3. Bi-weekly Progress Reports: Regular updates to keep everyone informed and ensure transparency throughout the project.
4. Final Report: A comprehensive final report, delivered at the project's conclusion, documenting the findings, proposed solutions, and recommendations.

Results and Value Added:

By applying the Design Thinking approach, we didn't just create innovative solutions; we made sure they were user-centered and sustainable. While the framework offers a clear structure, the real challenge was managing productive meetings, keeping everyone focused, and reading the room effectively. That's where my expertise, along with SkillShift Coaching©, proved invaluable.

Through my coaching, I guided the client in implementing, customizing, and scaling these strategies for long-term success. By integrating the GROWth Solution Mindset with the C.H.A.N.G.E. Framework for Doing the Right Things Right©—of which Design Thinking is a core element—we addressed immediate challenges and built enduring capabilities. This approach maintained momentum, overcame resistance, and ensured that solutions were practical, adaptable, and aligned with the client's long-term vision.

Conclusion:

This case study demonstrates how Design Thinking enabled my federal government client to tackle complex system challenges. By employing a structured yet flexible problem-solving approach, we ensured the solutions were desirable, technically feasible, and financially viable, driving meaningful and lasting change.

Consulting Case Study #6.
Transforming Executive Leadership Through Coaching

In the high-stakes environment of the federal government, executives at the Director and Director General levels often encounter significant challenges. My client, a Crown corporation in the financial sector, faced these very issues. Their executives were grappling with rapid policy changes, stakeholder relationship management, and public perception. Additionally, they needed to adapt to emerging technologies, drive innovation, and navigate an uncertain landscape.

I was tasked with helping them find a solution and provide targeted training that strengthened their decision-making, team-building, and emotional intelligence skills. By focusing on efficiency, innovation, stakeholder engagement and strategic decision-making, together we aimed to address their specific challenges and drive meaningful improvement.

This section shares a real-world case where my role as a Senior Leadership Development Consultant, using the GROWth Solution Mindset Coaching© framework, made a significant impact. An important aspect of our approach was the implementation of the "Coach the Coaches" concept. This involved training selected leaders to become internal coaches themselves, creating a sustainable coaching culture within the organization. By developing these internal coaches, we not only addressed immediate leadership needs but also built long-term capacity for ongoing development. This approach ensured that the executives could continue to support and mentor each other, driving continuous improvement and fostering a collaborative environment.

Tailored Executive Coaching.

My approach involved both individual and group coaching sessions, each tailored to address the specific needs of federal executives:

- **Individual Coaching Sessions:** We kicked off with detailed preliminary assessments through emails, phone calls, and virtual meetings. The goal was to create a supportive, non-judgmental space where executives could delve into their challenges and potential. With the GROWth Solution Mindset Coaching© framework, I helped each leader uncover hidden strengths and develop actionable strategies, while tracking their progress against clear milestones.

- **Group Coaching Sessions:** For group sessions, we used a dynamic structure that included presentations, group discussions, and individual reflections. This setup encouraged participants to explore habitual behaviors and discover new practices. The feedback we received was overwhelmingly positive, executives appreciated the focus on listening, questioning, and feedback, which built momentum and provided the tools needed to drive change within their teams.

The GROWth Solution Mindset Coaching© Framework in action.

The real standout was how the GROWth Solution Mindset Coaching© framework resonated with our client. Here's how it worked:

1. **Define the Winning Aspiration (Goal):** We began by defining a compelling vision that aligned with the team's goals. This vision acted as a North Star, guiding them from their current state to their desired future.
2. **Assess Current Reality (Reality):** We closely examined their current situation, identifying strengths and areas for improvement. Building a supportive network was crucial to provide guidance and resources throughout the process.
3. **Explore Options (Options):** Together, we explored various strategies, evaluating the best pathways to achieve their objectives. This involved assessing different approaches to find the most effective route.
4. **Set Inspirational Goals (Way Forward):** We crafted goals that were both challenging and motivating, focusing on solutions to keep the team inspired and moving forward. This helped ensure that the direction was clear and actionable.
5. **Create Time-Bound Action Plans (Time Horizon):** We developed specific, measurable, and time-bound action plans with clear deadlines. This SMART approach made goals attainable and progress easily trackable.
6. **Implement and Monitor:** We put the plans into action, continuously monitoring progress and adapting strategies as needed. A feedback-rich environment ensured alignment with the vision and responsiveness to any changes.

By following these steps, the GROWth Solution Mindset Coaching© framework drove meaningful and sustainable improvements, fostering a growth-oriented culture as the initiative gained momentum.

Coaching the Coaches.

The client was particularly impressed with the opportunity to cultivate internal coaching talent. They valued the structured approach provided by the GROWth Solution Mindset Coaching© framework, recognizing its potential to empower their leaders to become coaches themselves. This focus on developing internal coaches not only addressed immediate needs but also enhanced the organization's long-term capacity for leadership and development.

My hope is that this case illustrates how the GROWth Solution Mindset Coaching© framework, combined with my client's focus on building internal coaching capabilities, led to substantial improvements in executive performance and team dynamics. Through personalized coaching and a feedback-oriented approach, we achieved meaningful and sustainable advancements in federal leadership.

Your Next Steps to Becoming a Skillful Leader...

Now that you have a structured approach to transformation, integrating best practices from proven frameworks, a strategy that leverages strengths and resources rather than focusing solely on problem root causes, and a tailored delivery method for addressing specific client challenges with measurable outcomes, you might be wondering: What's next?

To further enrich your approach, let's explore a few additional strategies. These tried-and-tested models from four internationally recognized firms offer valuable insights that complement and enhance my signature framework.

McKinsey's "Inside-Out" leadership[45] emphasizes that effective leadership starts with self-awareness and personal development. **Ernst & Young's coaching approach**[46] underscores the importance of investing in managers by fostering psychological safety, creating a compelling team purpose, and preparing them for transformational leadership. **IDEO's Culture of Experimentation**[47] promotes rapid prototyping, iterative feedback, and learning from failures to drive innovation. **The Jobs to be Done (JTBD) Model**[48] focuses on understanding the specific goals executives are aiming to achieve, ensuring that coaching is tailored to address their real-world needs.

As you review these points, you'll likely recognize how they align with many aspects of my signature framework. This shows that my approach is up-to-date and consistent with leading thought leaders in the field.

Below is a brief summary of these models:

1. **McKinsey's 'Inside-Out' approach.**

McKinsey's "Inside-Out" leadership approach highlights that great leaders start with self-awareness and personal growth. When leaders are clear about their own values and strengths, they handle challenges better, communicate more effectively, and positively influence their teams and organizations.

The idea is simple: to lead others well, you first need to understand yourself. This means knowing your strengths, weaknesses, values, and motivations. When leaders work on developing themselves internally, they become more authentic and effective in guiding their teams and driving organizational change.

This approach contrasts with the "Outside-In" perspective, which focuses more on external factors like market conditions. Instead, "Inside-Out" leadership suggests that internal clarity and personal development are crucial for achieving broader leadership goals and making a real impact.

Beyond self-awareness, McKinsey's approach includes several other key elements:

1. **Authenticity:** Being true to yourself builds trust and credibility.
2. **Emotional Intelligence:** Understanding and managing your own emotions, and those of others, is crucial.
3. **Self-Reflection:** Regularly reflecting on your experiences helps you learn and improve.
4. **Personal Growth:** Continuous learning and adapting are essential for staying effective.
5. **Alignment with Organizational Values:** Ensuring your personal values align with your organization's mission creates consistency.
6. **Resilience and Adaptability:** Building resilience helps you handle setbacks and adapt to change.
7. **Role Modeling:** Setting a positive example reinforces the culture you want to create.

Overall, **"Inside-Out" leadership is about using personal insights and growth to lead in a way that truly resonates with others and drives positive results.** It's about aligning your personal purpose with your organization's goals, communicating authentically, building strong relationships, and creating a compelling vision that inspires your team.

2. **EY's Leader as a Coach approach (or Coaching approach to Leadership)**

Invest in managers themselves by taking a coaching approach.

What's the bottom line? If you want managers to lead transformation and drive change effectively, you've got to invest in them first. That means **adopting a coaching approach that prepares managers to navigate and lead change successfully.**

Here's how to get managers ready to guide their teams through change, even as things keep evolving:

1. **Slow Down to Speed Up:** When managers step into leadership roles, they need to build a team that's ready for success. The key? Creating a safe and open environment where everyone can communicate freely. Managers often need guidance on how to set this up. Taking time at the start of your transformation to focus on these basics can make a big difference. Don't rush through this; it's crucial for the long-term success of your change efforts.
2. **Create a Compelling Team Purpose:** People need a reason to embrace change. After a couple of years of unpredictable change, it's even more important to connect the change to a meaningful purpose. Research from EY shows that purpose-driven businesses outperform others. Managers need to understand how the change aligns with both individual and organizational goals. Help them grasp why the transformation is important and how it will boost productivity and impact. This isn't just about getting buy-in; it's about fostering a shared commitment.
3. **Have the Tough Conversations:** For change to be successful, it's essential to address how it affects your people. Think about potential conflicts, ways to resolve issues, and how to keep everyone engaged. Managers will need support in handling these aspects. Give them the space and tools to work through these challenges. Provide them with frameworks and guidance to build their confidence in leading their teams through the change.

By focusing on these principles, you'll help your managers become more effective leaders in times of transformation.

3. IDEO's Culture of experimentation

Here's a take on IDEO's Culture of Experimentation[49] and how it applies to executive coaching:

IDEO's Culture of Experimentation is all about embracing a mindset where trying out new ideas and learning from failures are part of the game. Instead of fearing mistakes, IDEO encourages teams to see them as valuable chances to learn and improve.

Here's how they do it:

1. **Rapid Prototyping:** Start with quick, simple versions of your ideas to test them out and get feedback.
2. **Iterative Design:** Keep tweaking and refining based on what you learn.
3. **Embracing Failure:** Treat failures as steppingstones to success, not setbacks.
4. **Collaboration and Openness:** Share ideas and insights freely across teams.

This approach helps organizations stay nimble and come up with solutions that really meet users' needs.

When we bring these ideas into executive coaching, they can make a big difference. Here's how:

1. **Encourage a Growth Mindset:** Just like IDEO, coaches can help leaders see challenges as chances to grow, not just hurdles.
2. **Experiment with Leadership Styles:** Try out different leadership strategies on a smaller scale before rolling them out. For example, a leader might test various communication styles with their team to see what works best.
3. **Iterate and Improve:** Use regular feedback to refine leadership practices. It's about learning and adjusting as you go.
4. **Learn from Failures:** Encourage leaders to view setbacks as learning opportunities. Analyze what went wrong and adjust strategies accordingly.
5. **Focus on Team Needs:** Help leaders understand and respond to their team's needs. Experiment with different ways to engage and support their teams based on direct feedback.
6. **Create a Safe Space for Ideas:** Make sure leaders feel comfortable trying out new approaches without fear of criticism.
7. **Cross-Disciplinary Learning:** Expose leaders to diverse perspectives and experiences to spark new ideas.
8. **Document and Reflect:** Encourage leaders to keep track of their experiments and reflections. This helps in understanding what works and what doesn't.
9. **Use Data and Feedback:** Help leaders use feedback and data to make informed decisions about their leadership strategies.

By integrating these principles into executive coaching, leaders can become more flexible, innovative, and effective, driving meaningful change and growth in their roles.

Be Bold: Embrace the Power of Experiments

IDEO's founder, David Kelley [24], emphasized that creating a culture of experimentation means shifting away from rigid planning and embracing a dynamic, adaptive approach. At its core, this culture is about accepting that failure is a part of the process—especially early on. When teams experiment, they can test ideas quickly, learn what works, and pivot without getting locked into one course. Kelley's view is clear: planning is overrated, and experimentation allows for flexibility and faster, more meaningful learning.

> *"An experiment, by definition, could go either way. That makes a completely different environment—one where people become open-minded, seeing new things."*
> —David Kelley, Founder of IDEO & Stanford D. School

This mindset fosters openness to failure, making it clear that mistakes are not setbacks but necessary steps toward discovery. Small failures early on provide valuable feedback, helping refine ideas before investing too heavily. In contrast, a heavy planning approach often stifles innovation, as it pressures teams to adhere to preconceived paths rather than adapting to real-world insights. The key is creating an environment where trying new things is encouraged, even if they don't always succeed immediately.

Kelley's approach aligns perfectly with how leaders can develop in executive coaching. Rather than meticulously planning every decision or strategy, leaders can experiment with different approaches—be it communication styles, leadership techniques, or team engagement strategies. By treating every attempt as an experiment, leaders can pivot, refine, and adapt more swiftly, ensuring that their strategies align with the evolving needs of their teams.

Additionally, building this culture requires psychological safety. Leaders must feel secure enough to try new methods without fear of judgment. This openness fosters creative problem-solving and cross-disciplinary thinking, as team members feel empowered to share and test diverse ideas.

By embracing experimentation, leaders become more resilient and adaptable, viewing challenges as opportunities to innovate rather than obstacles. The result is a more dynamic, flexible leadership style that aligns with real-world demands.

Are you ready to embrace this approach and see how it can transform your leadership style?

4. **Jobs to be Done Model (JTBD)**

The Jobs to be Done (JTBD) model **is all about figuring out what customers are really trying to achieve with products or services.** Instead of just looking at what people buy, this model focuses on the "jobs" they're hiring these products or services to do.

Here's a quick rundown of the JTBD model:

The model focuses on what people are trying to achieve with products or services. It helps you understand the specific tasks or goals customers have—whether they are practical, like commuting efficiently, or emotional, like feeling confident. By clearly defining these goals, you can design solutions that truly address their needs. This approach also reveals new opportunities for innovation and provides a broader perspective on competition by highlighting any solutions that might fulfill similar goals.

The JTBD model emphasizes understanding the real objectives behind customers' choices. Instead of just focusing on what they buy, it's about grasping the specific problems they need to solve or the feelings they want to achieve. This insight helps you tailor your offerings more effectively, uncover new opportunities for innovation, and stay ahead of competitors by identifying and addressing the underlying needs customers are looking to fulfill.

In summary, the JTBD model shifts the focus from simply what customers buy to why they make those choices. It helps you grasp the real goals they're trying to achieve—whether practical tasks or emotional needs. By understanding these deeper objectives, you can craft solutions that genuinely address their needs, uncover fresh innovation opportunities, and gain a competitive edge by identifying and meeting those underlying needs more effectively.

How the JTBD Model Can Boost Executive Coaching:

To make executive coaching more effective, **start by pinpointing the key goals and challenges the executive wants to address.** This involves understanding both their practical objectives—like developing a strategic plan—and their emotional needs—such as boosting confidence in decision-making. Once these goals are clear, use this insight to set specific, actionable coaching targets that align with the executive's desired outcomes.

Next, tailor your coaching methods to meet these specific goals. For example, if improving team dynamics is a focus, incorporate relevant exercises and strategies into your sessions. Regularly measure progress through feedback, performance metrics, and by addressing any gaps identified using the JTBD model. If traditional coaching methods fall short, consider alternative resources or specialized training to better meet the executive's needs.

In summary, applying the JTBD model helps ensure that coaching is directly relevant to the executive's core goals. This approach keeps coaching sessions focused, engaging, and adaptable, leading to more meaningful results and helping executives effectively tackle their real challenges

Bottom Line:

Now, you have all the elements to start your journey toward becoming a truly skillful leader—one who drives transformation with clarity, confidence, and impact. By embracing self-awareness, coaching your team through change, fostering a culture of experimentation, and aligning with your organization's goals, you are already on the path to making a significant difference. But remember, the road to great leadership is about continuous growth

Steps to Put This Into Practice:

1. **Start with Self-Awareness:** Take a page from McKinsey's "Inside-Out" approach—know yourself, understand your values, and let that clarity shape your leadership.
2. **Adopt a Coaching Mindset:** Apply EY's "Leader as a Coach" approach—build trust, align your team's purpose with the mission, and lead them through change with intention and compassion.
3. **Embrace Experimentation:** Follow IDEO's example by encouraging rapid testing of ideas, welcoming failure as part of learning, and iterating based on feedback.

4. **Focus on Real Needs:** Follow the JTBD model to tailor your leadership—understand the true goals of your team and your organization and craft your strategies around what matters most.
5. **Use the C.H.A.N.G.E. Framework:** Build your roadmap, set goals, and stay committed to doing the right things right—iterate as you move forward and ensure the whole organization understands and supports your transformation vision.
    - Start with a Minimum Viable Product or Service (MVP/MVS) to deliver early value and validate concepts. Implement a Minimum Variable Change (MVC) to make incremental adjustments, ensuring that each change is manageable and effective, enhancing the overall solution without overwhelming the system.
    - Finally, embrace the 8 mindsets and 8 frameworks as key tools for ongoing success. These mindsets, such as agility and resilience, and frameworks for problem-solving and planning, will enhance your leadership and foster a culture of growth and learning within your team.

By following these steps, you will not only guide your team through challenges but also become a leader who inspires growth and delivers lasting results.

Key Takeaways:

Integrate self-awareness, coaching, experimentation, and continuous learning to drive impactful and adaptive leadership.

1. Leadership starts with you — when you are clear on who you are, you lead with impact.
2. Coaching and building trust will help you guide your team through uncertainty.
3. Fostering a culture of experimentation drives agility and innovation.
4. Align your leadership with the specific needs of your team to maximize your influence.
5. A structured roadmap grounded in the C.H.A.N.G.E. Framework ensures your transformation efforts stay on track and deliver results.

Conclusion.

"The way to get started is to quit talking and begin doing."
— Walt Disney

Elevate Your Leadership Game Now!

You now have all the tools to transform your leadership and your organization. The strategies outlined in this book are designed to empower you to create real, lasting change and achieve significant results. By taking action on these steps, you'll build confidence and develop the skills to lead with clarity and purpose. If at any point you need further guidance, I'm available to help you accelerate your progress. My contact details are below—let's work together to save you time, energy, and resources while fast-tracking your success.

Leadership isn't about being perfect from the start; it's about growth. Just like learning a new skill, the more you practice and apply what you've learned, the more confident and capable you'll become. Your past experiences already give you a solid foundation—this book will help you leverage those strengths to lead with greater impact.

Transformation doesn't happen overnight, but with each step, you'll build competence, shed doubt, and accelerate your growth. Just like the heroes in stories, you'll evolve from uncertainty to confidence, from hesitation to mastery. And in doing so, you'll inspire those around you to unlock their potential as well.

The question isn't whether you're capable; it's whether you'll take action. Will you step up and embrace the leader you're meant to be? The outcome is in your hands. With focus and commitment, you can achieve extraordinary things.

So, why wait? Begin your transformation today.

For more tools to elevate your leadership, visit www.LearningSolutionsDelivery.com. Our seminars and resources are designed to help leaders like you succeed. Let's connect and help you build a successful career in transformation leadership.

Let's do this!

A Personal Reflection.

As you may have noticed, I have a great affinity for famous quotes because they make me reflect and value what is essential. As a parting thought, I'd like to share a quote I came up with some time ago that encapsulates my philosophy. It may sound a bit silly, but it has worked for me in life:

> "Life is like a round of golf. You must hit the ball from wherever your last shot landed, and still aim for the best possible outcome."

To me, this quote conveys several key insights:

Adaptability: Just like in golf, life requires you to adapt to your current circumstances. You can't always control where you end up, but you must make the best of it.

Persistence: The idea of aiming for the best possible outcome despite setbacks emphasizes the importance of perseverance. Every shot, regardless of its outcome, is an opportunity to learn and improve.

Focus on the Process: The quote encourages a focus on the present moment and the process rather than dwelling on past mistakes. Each shot is a chance to refocus and adjust your approach.

Realism: It reflects the reality that life is not always perfect, and you must work with what you have, making the best decisions from your current position.

Goal Orientation: The mention of aiming for the best possible outcome underscores the importance of having goals and aspirations, even when faced with challenges.

Overall, it's a reminder that how you respond to setbacks can shape your journey and influence your ultimate success. I hope this perspective resonates with you and offers some value on your journey.

About the Author.

With over two decades of experience driving transformative change, Joel Velázquez has consistently delivered measurable results across industries. His multilingual abilities have enabled him to collaborate with diverse clients worldwide, while his background in economics and certifications—PMP, Prosci, APMG, ICAgile, and advanced Design Thinking from IDEO—equip him to lead teams through complex transformations. Whether in private or public sector organizations, Joel's expertise ensures success even in the most challenging environments.

Career Journey

Before founding his coaching and consulting business in Canada, Joel held various roles at multinational companies like Ford Motor Company, American Express, Xerox Corporation, and Nortel Networks. During his time there, he saw firsthand the challenges organizations face when trying to implement meaningful change.

This experience ignited his passion for creating lasting, positive change, which led him to launch Learning Solutions Delivery Inc. and Solutions Delivery PM Services Inc. Through these firms, Joel has consistently enhanced operational efficiency, streamlined workflows, and delivered transformative learning programs that have empowered hundreds of employees and leaders to achieve measurable success.

Approach

Joel stands out for his ability to integrate proven methodologies like Agile Coaching, Lean Change Management, and Design Thinking into actionable, real-world solutions. He collaborates closely with organizations to streamline workflows, boost operational efficiency, and foster a culture of continuous learning, all while staying aligned with the company's unique objectives.

Clients consistently praise him for delivering projects on time and within budget, and for cultivating innovation and ongoing improvement. His deep expertise in navigating transformational change not only brings immediate results but also lays the groundwork for long-term success. With his hands-on, practical approach, Joel empowers clients to confidently manage complex transitions, making him a reliable partner in driving lasting impact.

Why Clients Work with Him

Joel takes a hands-on, results-driven approach. His clients value that he doesn't just offer advice—he actively collaborates with them to implement changes that stick. Whether it's transforming processes, boosting employee engagement, or adopting new technologies, he focuses on creating meaningful, lasting impact.

Through his SkillShift Coaching© and CHANGE Framework for Doing the Right Things Right©, Joel helps leaders and teams navigate change successfully. Its framework equips organizations to tackle the challenges arising from any transformation in a structured and systematic way.

Joel lives in Ottawa, Canada, with his wife and two young adult children. When he is not advising or coaching any of his corporate clients, he's constantly learning and refining his methods to ensure he remains at the forefront of the industry. If you're ready to explore how Joel can help your organization achieve its goals, feel free to reach out to him at joel.velazquez@solutions-delivery.ca

Index

A

Accountability 28, 70, 83, 117, 121
Action orientation 108
Active engagement xix, 89
Adaptability xxi, xxiv, xxvi, 8, 20, 22, 24, 26, 44, 45, 51, 54, 65, 68, 78, 100, 107, 108, 118, 119, 141, 150, 159, 171, 172
Additional strategies 149
Adjustment 24, 26, 46, 58, 83, 85, 88, 91, 92, 93, 94, 111, 117, 119, 121, 128, 132, 136, 137, 156
Adkar model 55, 137
Adoption rate 90
Advanced courses and research xvii
Advisors vii, 83, 106, 107, 109, 110, 111, 112, 120, 121
Agile methodology 15, 53, 85, 95, 108, 118, 119
Agile practices 44, 45, 52, 53, 54, 85, 98, 100, 119, 120, 140
Agility xxi, xxii, xxvi, 51, 53, 54, 73, 74, 75, 85, 117, 141, 156
Agility and innovation 156
Aligning frameworks and processes 96
Alignment 6, 19, 33, 39, 42, 45, 46, 49, 52, 53, 59, 64, 71, 81, 83, 87, 92, 93, 94, 95, 96, 97, 98, 109, 110, 111, 120, 121, 138, 139, 140, 141, 147, 150
Alignment with organizational values 150
Applying systems thinking 66
Architectural design 126

Assessing readiness for change 55, 58

B

Balanced scorecard 96
Behavioral indicators 91
Benchmarking 91, 93, 94
Best practices 1, 30, 55, 60, 87, 93, 98, 118, 139, 142, 149
Blueprint xv, xvii, 104, 109, 111, 123, 126, 134, 135, 136
Budget concerns xi
Bureaucratic frustration x
Bureaucratic inertia 82
Business administration 113
Business needs 88
Business transformation i, ix, xiv, xix, 3, 7, 108

C

Canadian public sector ix, 25, 26, 27, 28, 29, 81, 82, 84, 85, 86, 87
Capability owners 108, 109, 110
Case studies 37, 43, 61, 66, 70, 71, 82, 84, 96
Challenges vii, xi, xiii, xiv, xv, xvii, xviii, xix, xxi, xxii, xxiii, xxiv, 1, 3, 4, 6, 7, 11, 14, 15, 16, 19, 20, 22, 25, 27, 30, 31, 35, 36, 37, 39, 41, 45, 53, 54, 56, 58, 59, 60, 62, 63, 65, 66, 69, 70, 71, 72, 73, 74, 75, 76, 78, 80, 81, 82, 83, 88, 90, 96, 98, 100, 103, 106, 108, 111, 113, 117, 120, 121, 126, 136, 138,

141, 142, 144, 145, 146, 149, 151, 152, 154, 155, 156, 159, 160, 161
Challenges and opportunities xxii, 11, 22
Change agents 61, 109, 111
Change champions 60, 108, 109, 111
Change evangelists 109
C.H.A.N.G.E. Framework for Doing the Right Things Right© xiv, 1, 113, 114, 121, 123, 134, 135, 137, 138, 142, 145
Change management xiii, xiv, 11, 39, 45, 46, 49, 53, 54, 55, 56, 58, 59, 60, 61, 65, 85, 89, 96, 100, 108, 109, 120, 160, 175
Change management strategies xiii, 53, 61, 65
C.H.A.N.G.E. Process© 14, 15, 110, 111
Change sponsors 108, 109, 110
Choose wisely 103
Citizen experience 3, 4, 6, 8
Clarified goals 117
Clarity and direction xiii
Clarity and focus 107
Clarity in roles 112
Clear mission 3, 4
Clear vision 8, 9, 11, 16, 56, 116, 137
Client challenges 142, 149
Client satisfaction 135
Coaching mindset 24, 28, 29, 75, 78, 82, 101, 155
Coaching mindset approach 29, 75, 82
Coach the coaches 146
Collaboration xiii, xxv, 15, 20, 23, 24, 28, 30, 31, 36, 44, 45, 53, 55, 67, 68, 69, 70, 78, 87, 100, 113, 119, 138, 139, 140, 141, 144, 152, 173
Collaboration and communication xiii
Collaborative problem-solving 31
Commitment xi, xviii, xxvi, 5, 7, 27, 36, 55, 60, 65, 70, 72, 73, 78, 83, 89, 94, 123, 151, 157, 173
Common leadership challenges xix
Communication xiii, xxi, xxv, 15, 19, 20, 36, 44, 56, 59, 60, 61, 67, 68, 69, 83, 89, 92, 93, 100, 101, 113, 120, 132, 139, 140, 141, 144, 152, 153

Community impact 5
Comparative analysis 91
Compelling team purpose 149, 151
Complex challenges xiii, xxiv, 30, 62, 63, 81
Complexity and change 81
Connecting the dots 92, 137
Consulting case study 15, 36, 74, 113, 135, 138, 142, 146
Consulting engagement 113
Continuous feedback 82, 85, 141
Continuous growth xviii, 155
Continuous improvement 22, 24, 29, 33, 36, 38, 39, 41, 42, 43, 53, 65, 70, 83, 109, 117, 141, 146
Continuous learning xxii, xxvi, 24, 29, 69, 75, 78, 101, 150, 156, 161, 174
Continuous planning and adaptation 45
Corporate management directorate 113, 135
Critical decision-making 119
Cross-departmental collaboration 36
Cross-functional collaboration 31
Cross-functional teams 15, 45, 52, 117, 140
Crown corporation 83, 146
Cultural barriers 42
Cultural shift 78, 82
Cultural transformation 28, 78
Culture of resilience 8
Current reality 80, 139, 140, 147
Current state 11, 15, 58, 80, 88, 137, 138, 139, 147
Customer satisfaction 25, 41, 43, 44, 93, 172
Cybersecurity measures 4, 7, 9

D

Daily stand-up meetings 45
Dare model 107, 109, 111, 112
Data security xi, 3, 4, 6, 7, 8, 9
Data security concerns xi
Data security measures 6
Deciders 107, 108, 109, 110, 111, 120, 121

Decision levels 104
Decision making 95, 104, 120
Decision-making framework 107, 120
Defining the change vision and objectives 56
Design for strategy 63, 64, 71, 72, 73, 74, 75, 87, 101, 118, 119
Design thinking 30, 31, 33, 35, 36, 37, 38, 59, 63, 64, 71, 72, 74, 75, 84, 85, 87, 98, 100, 117, 139, 140, 142, 143, 145, 160, 171, 175
Developing a change management plan 56, 58
Digital portal 126, 128, 135, 136
Digital transformation 3, 73, 82
Distributed decision-making blueprint 104, 109, 111
Diversity and inclusion 83
Document and reflect 152
Double diamond process 31, 33

E

Education 84, 89
Effective business transformation 7
Effective leadership xxi, xxii, xxiii, xxv, xxvi, 12, 29, 60, 67, 70, 149
Effectiveness xvii, xxiii, xxiv, 1, 26, 36, 37, 39, 42, 51, 53, 58, 60, 61, 67, 68, 71, 72, 73, 75, 86, 88, 96, 98, 100, 103, 104, 110, 114, 117, 119, 138, 140, 141
Effectiveness and efficiency 100, 103, 104, 140, 141
Efficiency 1, 7, 8, 26, 36, 38, 39, 41, 43, 44, 49, 51, 54, 55, 69, 73, 74, 83, 84, 87, 93, 98, 100, 101, 103, 104, 111, 112, 113, 116, 117, 119, 121, 134, 135, 136, 137, 140, 141, 146, 160, 161, 173
Eight mindsets xvii
Embracing failure 152
Emotional intelligence xxv, xxvi, 67, 68, 69, 70, 71, 86, 98, 101, 119, 120, 146, 150
Empathy and user-centricity 36
Employee empowerment 75
Employee engagement 29, 41, 55, 61, 82, 94, 161, 174
Employee net promoter score 91
Empowerment across levels 112
Empowerment through knowledge xix
Engagement xix, xxii, xxiii, 5, 23, 25, 29, 30, 36, 41, 55, 58, 61, 73, 74, 75, 82, 89, 90, 91, 94, 107, 109, 113, 128, 140, 146, 153, 161, 173, 174
Engaging stakeholders 56
Enhanced quality 44
Ensuring alignment 42, 49, 52, 71, 92, 109, 110, 120
Ensuring alignment with existing processes 92
Ensuring staff buy-in 89
Enterprise architecture as strategy 95
E-shaped people xxiv
Evaluate progress 33, 45, 58, 59, 111
Executive leadership 83, 146
Executors 107, 108, 109, 111, 112, 120, 121
Expectations 23, 44, 89
Experimentation 28, 53, 65, 72, 74, 117, 149, 151, 153, 154, 155, 156, 176
Explore options 107, 139, 147
External advice 88

F

Federal health sector 113, 138
Feedback xxv, xxvi, 20, 25, 26, 28, 31, 35, 37, 41, 44, 45, 52, 55, 56, 58, 59, 62, 63, 64, 66, 69, 72, 74, 80, 81, 82, 83, 85, 87, 90, 93, 94, 108, 109, 111, 113, 117, 119, 128, 130, 132, 136, 137, 139, 141, 144, 147, 148, 149, 152, 153, 155, 172
Feedback mechanisms 113
Finish line 7, 8, 116
Fiscal responsibility 4
Flexibility xxiv, 20, 23, 24, 44, 49, 51, 107, 108, 153
Flexibility and adaptability 20, 44, 51
Focus ix, xxii, xxiii, xxiv, xxvi, 1, 5, 6, 7, 15, 19, 22, 23, 31, 38, 39, 44, 49, 62, 66, 71, 76, 81, 83, 90, 98, 100, 103, 106, 107, 108, 110, 111, 112, 118, 121,

135, 141, 142, 147, 148, 151, 152, 154, 155, 156, 157, 159, 172
Focus groups 90
Focus on real needs 156
The Four Pillars 17, 118
Fragmentation 116
Framework vii, ix, x, xi, xiii, xiv, xv, xvii, xviii, xix, xxi, 1, 5, 11, 14, 15, 22, 28, 29, 30, 37, 39, 45, 49, 51, 52, 54, 55, 56, 58, 62, 63, 64, 66, 67, 71, 72, 74, 75, 76, 78, 81, 82, 83, 84, 85, 87, 88, 89, 90, 91, 92, 93, 94, 95, 96, 97, 98, 100, 101, 104, 107, 108, 109, 111, 112, 113, 114, 117, 118, 119, 120, 121, 123, 133, 134, 135, 137, 138, 139, 140, 141, 142, 143, 145, 146, 147, 148, 149, 151, 156, 161, 174, 175
Frameworks vii, ix, x, xi, xiii, xiv, xv, xvii, xviii, xix, xxi, 1, 5, 11, 14, 15, 22, 28, 29, 30, 37, 39, 45, 49, 51, 52, 54, 55, 56, 58, 62, 63, 64, 66, 67, 71, 72, 74, 75, 76, 78, 81, 82, 83, 84, 85, 87, 88, 89, 90, 91, 92, 93, 94, 95, 96, 97, 98, 100, 101, 104, 107, 108, 109, 111, 112, 113, 114, 117, 118, 119, 120, 121, 123, 133, 134, 135, 137, 138, 139, 140, 141, 142, 143, 145, 146, 147, 148, 149, 151, 156, 161, 174, 175
Frameworks and models ix

G

Gap analysis 11, 14, 117
Goals xiii, xvii, xviii, xxiii, xxiv, xxv, 3, 4, 6, 7, 11, 14, 15, 16, 22, 23, 24, 33, 35, 36, 37, 39, 42, 46, 49, 53, 56, 58, 59, 60, 63, 67, 68, 69, 71, 72, 74, 75, 78, 80, 81, 82, 83, 88, 93, 94, 95, 96, 98, 100, 101, 103, 104, 106, 108, 109, 110, 111, 112, 113, 116, 117, 118, 119, 120, 121, 123, 126, 128, 134, 137, 139, 140, 146, 147, 149, 150, 151, 154, 155, 156, 159, 161, 174
Governance 104, 111, 112
GROW Model 29, 75, 78, 175

Growth Mindset 28, 29, 76, 78, 82, 152, 174, 175
GROWTH Mindset 28, 29, 76, 78, 82, 152, 174, 175
Growth-oriented culture 147

H

High-level vision 123
Holistic development 78
How change management works 55
How emotional intelligence works 67
How systems thinking works 62
Human impact 7, 8, 139

I

IDEO's Culture of Experimentation 149, 151
Implementation 12, 23, 24, 31, 53, 54, 58, 59, 60, 65, 70, 81, 82, 85, 86, 88, 91, 92, 104, 106, 107, 108, 109, 110, 111, 112, 117, 120, 123, 128, 130, 132, 136, 137, 141, 146
Implementation decisions 106
Implementation focus 108
Implementation layer 111, 128
Implementing the change 56, 58
Improved collaboration 44
Improved implementation 112
Improvement 1, 15, 22, 24, 29, 33, 36, 38, 39, 41, 42, 43, 44, 45, 46, 53, 58, 60, 61, 62, 65, 69, 70, 73, 80, 83, 84, 88, 90, 91, 93, 94, 96, 109, 113, 114, 117, 120, 128, 132, 137, 139, 141, 146, 147, 148, 161
Incentives 89
Increased productivity 44
Inefficiencies 15, 42, 70, 73, 113, 116, 117, 118
Innovation xi, xiii, xxiii, xxiv, xxv, 1, 7, 15, 24, 25, 27, 28, 30, 36, 37, 38, 39, 41, 43, 44, 45, 52, 53, 62, 63, 65, 69, 71, 73, 74, 75, 81, 83, 87, 113, 118, 121, 142, 146, 149, 153, 154, 156, 161, 171, 174, 176
Innovative solutions 11, 20, 22, 31, 71, 72, 75, 117, 121, 145

Inspirational goals 80, 82, 83, 140, 147
Integration 4, 7, 36, 69, 71, 88, 92, 93, 94, 112, 126, 135
Integration and efficiency 7
Internal coaches 138, 146, 148
Interoperability challenges xi
Introducing a proven change management cycle 55
Invest in managers 150
Involvement 55, 72, 89
Iterative design 152
Iterative development 44, 45, 52, 87, 100, 118
Iterative value 128
ITIL® Practitioner Guidance 96

J

Jobs to be Done Model 154

K

Key concepts 66, 108
Key milestones 123, 124, 135
Key performance indicators 42, 93, 96
Key takeaway xix, xxvi, 6, 8, 16, 91, 93, 94, 103, 112, 140, 156
Knowledge broker xvii
Knowledge into action 137

L

Lasting impact 121, 161
Latin America vii
Leadership vii, ix, x, xiii, xiv, xvii, xix, xxi, xxii, xxiii, xxv, xxvi, 12, 15, 16, 29, 36, 53, 55, 60, 67, 68, 70, 73, 78, 82, 83, 97, 136, 139, 141, 146, 148, 149, 150, 151, 152, 153, 154, 155, 156, 157, 158, 171, 172, 174, 175, 176
Leadership choices ix
Leadership culture 78
Leadership development 82, 97, 146, 174
Leadership framework xiii, xix
Leadership in transformation x
Leadership models 82
Leadership principles 174
Leadership strategies 29, 152
Lean change management approach 108
Lean principles 38, 39, 41, 42, 43, 54, 84, 98, 100, 118, 119, 120
Leveraging this structured approach 56
Long-term success 7, 22, 71, 119, 145, 151, 161

M

Managing organizational alignment 96
Manufacturing vii, 26, 38, 43
Mapping 35, 37, 39, 41, 62, 74, 92
McKinsey's "Inside-Out" Leadership 149, 175
Meaningful improvement 36, 70, 146
Measurable outcomes 76, 149
Measuring impact 82, 97
Measuring progress xiii
Measuring staff satisfaction 90
Measuring success 93
Measuring success of alignment efforts 93
Minimum Viable Change 128, 132, 137
Minimum Viable Product 123, 128, 136, 156
Minimum Viable Service 128, 130, 136
Miracle Question 76
Mission Possible 3, 4, 6, 116
Models ii, ix, xiv, xvii, xix, xxi, xxii, xxiii, 29, 55, 61, 63, 64, 73, 75, 78, 82, 87, 101, 104, 106, 107, 108, 109, 111, 112, 113, 119, 126, 130, 132, 135, 136, 137, 138, 149, 154, 155, 156, 174, 175
Modernization efforts 36, 75
Modern Leadership xxvi
M-shaped People xxiii, xxiv, xxv
Multinational corporations xvii

N

Navigate obstacles 58, 111
Next steps 149

O

OKRs 117, 141
Operational complexities 113
Operations and digital innovation division 142
Opportunity identification 120
Organizational change 37, 61, 66, 96, 150, 175
Organizational culture 55, 78, 113
Outcomes vii, xv, xix, xxii, xxiv, xxv, 5, 7, 8, 9, 11, 14, 15, 22, 23, 24, 31, 46, 49, 51, 53, 55, 56, 58, 60, 63, 74, 76, 78, 84, 87, 88, 92, 100, 104, 106, 108, 109, 112, 117, 119, 120, 121, 123, 126, 128, 133, 134, 135, 136, 137, 142, 149, 155, 157, 159, 174
Outdated systems 113, 139
Outreach strategy 144
Ownership 41, 52, 55, 72, 89, 107, 141

P

Peer influence 89
Performance measurement 96
Personal development 149, 150
Personal growth 78, 149, 150, 175
Pilot frameworks 88
Piloting 92, 93, 132, 136
Pilot programs 130
Planning 22, 37, 45, 51, 52, 53, 54, 55, 58, 74, 75, 82, 95, 104, 112, 153, 156, 176
Political backlash fear xi
Positive organizational impact 78
Potential impact 24, 88, 95
Prioritization 23, 95
Prioritizing frameworks 88
Problem-solving xxi, xxii, xxiv, xxvi, 19, 20, 22, 23, 24, 25, 30, 31, 44, 61, 84, 87, 143, 145, 153, 156
Processes x, 3, 4, 7, 8, 9, 25, 26, 28, 33, 36, 38, 39, 41, 42, 45, 53, 55, 60, 61, 65, 69, 70, 73, 84, 87, 88, 92, 93, 94, 95, 96, 97, 100, 107, 108, 110, 113, 116, 117, 119, 126, 132, 135, 136, 138, 139, 140, 141, 161, 173, 174

Process realignment 137
Progress reports 141, 144
Project success metrics 94
Proven frameworks 30, 84, 98, 118, 139, 142, 149
Public accountability 83
Public and private sector vii

Q

Quality control vii

R

RACI Model 107
Rapid prototyping 31, 149, 152
Recognition 82, 89
Recommended reading 95
Regular reviews and retrospectives 45
Regulatory uncertainty xi
Related literature 37, 43, 54, 61, 66, 70, 75, 83
Research frameworks 88
Resilience xxiii, 8, 24, 27, 65, 66, 67, 68, 78, 86, 109, 141, 150, 156
Resistance xi, xiii, xix, 15, 36, 42, 53, 54, 55, 60, 61, 65, 89, 100, 113, 120, 132, 139, 141, 145
Resistance to change xix, 36, 42, 53, 54, 60, 61, 65, 113, 120, 132, 139
Resource allocation 4, 23, 56, 72, 74, 75, 82, 113, 140
Resource availability 88
Resource mobilization 16
Resource-oriented questions 76
Resources ix, xi, xiii, 4, 5, 6, 8, 11, 14, 15, 16, 22, 23, 26, 29, 38, 42, 53, 54, 56, 58, 59, 60, 61, 66, 69, 71, 72, 74, 75, 76, 81, 82, 88, 95, 98, 100, 103, 106, 109, 110, 113, 117, 118, 119, 120, 121, 123, 134, 139, 140, 142, 147, 149, 155, 157, 158, 172, 173, 175, 176
Review ii, 1, 45, 49, 87, 93, 94, 149, 171, 174, 175
Roadmap xvii, 14, 16, 46, 49, 94, 119, 123, 134, 135, 156

Role modeling 150

S

Satisfaction 3, 4, 6, 9, 25, 30, 41, 43, 44, 90, 91, 93, 94, 132, 135, 172
Scaling questions 76
Scrum teams & SMEs 109
Seamless decision flow 112
Secret sauce xvii
Self-awareness 67, 69, 101, 149, 150, 155, 156
Self-reflection 150, 175
Service delivery 3, 26, 36, 37, 42, 53, 65, 69, 70, 73, 74, 75, 87, 113, 117, 126, 135, 136, 137
Service delivery model 73, 126, 135, 136
Service design framework 37
Simplified leadership framework xix
Skill development xxii
Skill profiles xxiv
Skills and knowledge xiv, 89, 93
SMART Action Plans 140
Solution focused model 75, 78, 101, 175
Specifications 126
Stakeholder engagement 5, 58, 73, 74, 75, 146, 173
Stakeholders xiii, 5, 11, 19, 20, 23, 24, 27, 28, 36, 44, 45, 52, 53, 54, 55, 56, 58, 59, 64, 65, 72, 73, 74, 75, 92, 93, 94, 106, 107, 108, 111, 117, 121, 123, 136, 138, 139, 142, 144, 146, 173
Strategic alignment 46, 96
Strategic decisions 28, 71, 75, 106, 146, 174
Strategic direction 72, 109, 110, 116, 121, 139
Strategic focus 5
Strategic goals 59, 63, 71, 72, 101, 103, 104, 106, 108, 110, 111, 112, 116, 119, 120, 134
Strategic guidance 123
Strategic layer 110
Strategic vision 113, 116, 121, 126, 135, 141
Strategies x, xiii, xiv, xvii, xix, xxv, 1, 14, 15, 28, 29, 38, 44, 53, 56, 59, 60, 61, 63, 64, 65, 67, 70, 73, 75, 80, 81, 83, 84, 86, 88, 95, 96, 100, 103, 106, 110, 117, 133, 138, 141, 145, 146, 147, 149, 152, 153, 155, 156, 157
Strategy x, xiii, xiv, xvii, xix, xxv, 1, 14, 15, 20, 26, 28, 29, 38, 43, 44, 53, 56, 59, 60, 61, 63, 64, 65, 67, 70, 71, 72, 73, 74, 75, 78, 80, 81, 83, 84, 86, 87, 88, 94, 95, 96, 100, 101, 103, 106, 110, 111, 117, 118, 119, 120, 121, 133, 138, 139, 141, 142, 144, 145, 146, 147, 149, 152, 153, 155, 156, 157, 173, 174, 176
Strengths and resources 76, 142, 149
Structural racism 82, 83
Structured approach 11, 16, 55, 56, 71, 74, 104, 106, 121, 137, 143, 148, 149
Structured roadmap 156
Success metrics 94
Support requests 90
Surveys 35, 60, 90, 144
Sustainability and inclusivity concerns xi
Sustainable coaching culture 146
Sustainable success 78, 121, 134
Systems ii, xi, 3, 7, 15, 24, 26, 38, 61, 62, 63, 64, 65, 66, 69, 84, 85, 86, 87, 96, 100, 113, 118, 126, 128, 135, 136, 137, 139, 141, 142, 144, 145, 156, 172, 173
Systems thinking 61, 62, 63, 64, 65, 66, 86, 100, 118

T

T ix, xvii, xxi, xxiii, xxiv, xxv, 15, 22, 24, 27, 30, 43, 49, 67, 137, 145, 151, 152, 153, 157, 159, 161, 171, 175
Tactical decisions 106
Tactical layer 110
Tactical plan 126, 135
Tailored delivery 149
Talent and skills shortage x
Tangible outcomes xxiv, 108, 123, 128, 135
Team culture 80, 141
Team dynamics 78, 103, 148, 155

Team needs 67, 152
Technological complexity 36
Three layers of decision making 104
Time-bound action plans 80, 140, 147
Tough conversations 151
Training xiv, 42, 53, 56, 59, 60, 69, 82, 83, 84, 86, 89, 90, 93, 124, 136, 146, 155
Transformation i, vii, ix, x, xi, xiv, xv, xix, 1, 3, 4, 6, 7, 8, 11, 14, 15, 16, 28, 37, 73, 78, 82, 83, 88, 104, 108, 112, 113, 117, 118, 119, 120, 121, 123, 126, 128, 132, 133, 134, 135, 136, 137, 138, 139, 141, 142, 149, 150, 151, 155, 156, 157, 158, 160, 161
Transformational leadership x, 149
Transformation journey xi, xv, 1, 15, 123, 141
Transformation process 16, 119, 133, 135, 141
Transformative leadership xiii
Trial and error xvii
Tricks of the trade 88
Trust and satisfaction 6, 9

U

Understanding vii, xxi, xxiii, xxiv, 1, 3, 7, 11, 19, 20, 22, 23, 24, 30, 35, 36, 37, 38, 45, 52, 53, 55, 58, 59, 62, 63, 66, 68, 69, 71, 74, 85, 88, 89, 92, 93, 114, 118, 123, 130, 143, 149, 150, 152, 154, 155, 175
Use Data 152
User-centered solutions 30, 74
User experience 25, 26, 87, 90, 173
User feedback 31, 35, 87, 130

V

Value proposition 5, 116
Value stream mapping 39
Variable transformation outcomes xix
Vision xiii, 7, 8, 9, 11, 12, 14, 16, 27, 46, 49, 51, 52, 56, 58, 59, 72, 74, 80, 83, 98, 113, 116, 120, 121, 123, 126, 135, 137, 138, 139, 140, 141, 145, 147, 150, 156

W

Why Change Management Matters 54
Workflow Changes 126, 136
Workforce Resistance xi

Bibliography & References.

1. Mumford, C. C., Zaccaro, D. W., & Harding, C. A. (2000). Leadership skills: Competency-based approaches. Journal of Applied Psychology, 85(1), 102-113. https://doi.org/10.1037/0021-9010.85.1.102
2. Katz, R. L. (1955). Skills of an effective administrator. Harvard Business Review, 33(1), 33-42.
3. Mumford, Michael D. Leadership Skills for a Changing World. SAGE Publications, 2000.
4. Tim Brown from IDEO. "T-shaped people: The Importance of Versatility in Design Thinking." Retrieved from an article published on IDEO's website (2010) that discusses the "T-shaped people" concept and its relevance in design thinking and innovation.
5. Here's a brief explanation for why each example was chosen to represent its respective category:
    - 5.1. Tim Berners-Lee as an example of a T-shaped individual: Tim Berners-Lee, the inventor of the World Wide Web, exemplifies the balance between specialized skill and broad experience. His specialized skill in computer science, particularly in the development of web technologies, is evident. Additionally, his contributions have had a profound impact on a wide range of fields and industries, reflecting his broader experiences and competencies.
    - 5.2. Benjamin Franklin as an example of an M-shaped individual: Benjamin Franklin was a polymath who excelled in various fields, including science, politics, diplomacy, and literature. His diverse range of specialties and accomplishments highlight his versatility and adaptability, making him an exemplary M-shaped individual.
    - 5.3. Albert Einstein as an example of an I-shaped individual: Albert Einstein is renowned for his deep expertise in theoretical physics, particularly for his groundbreaking work on the theory of relativity. While his contributions to physics are profound, they primarily

reflect his specialization in a specific area rather than a breadth of experience in other domains.
5.4. Marie Curie as an example of a P-shaped individual: Marie Curie made significant contributions to the fields of physics and chemistry, particularly in the study of radioactivity. Her expertise in scientific research exemplifies her specialized skill, while her ability to apply her knowledge across different fields demonstrates versatility and adaptability, aligning with the characteristics of a P-shaped individual.
5.5. Leonardo da Vinci as an example of an E-shaped individual: Leonardo da Vinci was a true Renaissance man, excelling not only in art but also in various scientific disciplines such as engineering, anatomy, and mathematics. His wide-ranging interests and accomplishments showcase his combination of experience, expertise, exploration, and execution, making him an ideal example of an E-shaped individual.

6. Why Leadership is Not About Having All the Answers by Tim Brown, CEO of IDEO. March 2024 Newsletter
7. op Executives Need Feedback—Here's How They Can Get It by Robert S. Kaplan. McKinsey Quarterly September 1, 2011
8. Wayne Walter Dyer was an American self-help author and a motivational speaker. Books: Meditations for Manifesting, The Power of Intention, Wishes Fulfilled, among others.
9. Stone, Brad (2013). The Everything Store: Jeff Bezos and the Age of Amazon. Little, Brown and Company. This comprehensive biography of Jeff Bezos and Amazon delves into the company's origins and its relentless focus on customer satisfaction.
10. Knowledge at Wharton. Peter Fader (2020). How Starbucks came a long way on customer centricity. Wharton School Press. This article discusses Starbucks' journey towards becoming a more customer-centric company.
11. Immigration, Refugees and Citizenship Canada (IRCC) (2022). "Modernizing Canada's Immigration System to Support Economic Recovery and Improve Client Experience." https://www.canada.ca/en/immigration-refugees-citizenship/news/2022/01/modernizing-canadas-immigration-system-to-support-economic-recovery-and-improve-client-experience.html
12. Monden, Yasuhiro. (1994). Toyota Production System: An Integrated Approach to Just-in-Time. Institute of Industrial Engineers.
13. Walmart's inventory management system is a prime example of optimizing resources through advanced data analytics (inventoryy.com, 2023)

14. The Canada Revenue Agency (CRA) has adopted a digital-first approach for tax filings, streamlining processes and reducing paperwork. By harnessing digital technologies, such as online forms and automated systems, the CRA has optimized resource utilization, leading to heightened efficiency and cost savings. (Source: Canada Revenue Agency, Digital Services at the Canada Revenue Agency, 2023). https://www.canada.ca/en/revenue-agency/services/e-services.html
15. "Linzmayer, Owen. (2004). Apple Confidential: The Untold Story of Steve Jobs' Return to Apple. Crown Business. Kahney, Leander. (2013). Inside Steve's Brain: The Secret Lives of the Man Who Made Apple. Crown Business."
16. Outsource Accelerator, 2021. Nike: Outsourcing Strategy. Nike embraces a strategy of iterative product launches, strategically introducing new designs throughout the year. https://www.outsourceaccelerator.com
17. Public Services and Procurement Canada. (2023). "Outsourcing Strategy: A Glance at Our Plans 2023-2024." https://www.tpsgc-pwgsc.gc.ca/rapports-reports/pm-dp/2023-2024/
18. In response to the growing demand for healthier beverages and concerns about sugar intake, Coca-Cola launched Coca-Cola Zero Sugar, a reformulated version of its original soda with zero sugar and calories. (source: Coca-Cola Company). https://www.coca-colacompany.com/
19. Neil Patel, 2023. How Airbnb Uses Data to Improve User Experience. https://neilpatel.com/blog/how-airbnb-uses-data-science/
20. Health Canada's Health Products and Food Branch (HPFB) fosters stakeholder engagement through public consultations and advisory committees. Health Canada, "Consultations and Collaborations"). https://www.canada.ca/en/health-canada/corporate/about-health-canada/public-engagement.html
21. By offering a comprehensive suite of sustainable energy solutions, Tesla seeks to accelerate the transition to a cleaner and greener world (Tesla Inc., n.d.) (source: Tesla). https://www.tesla.com/en_ca
22. Patagonia's commitment to sustainability extends beyond product production. They advocate for environmental conservation and social responsibility, engaging in initiatives like the '1% for the Planet' program and promoting fair labor practices. (Source: Patagonia's Approach to Sustainability, 2023) https://www.patagonia.com/our-footprint/
23. Environment and Climate Change Canada (ECCC) formulates comprehensive climate action plans to achieve significant greenhouse gas emissions reductions and adapt to the impacts of climate change (ECCC, n.d.) (Source: Environment and Climate Change Canada, "Climate

Action"). https://www.canada.ca/en/environment-climate-change/services/climate-change/federal-sustainable-development-strategy/goals/climate-action.html
24. Google encourages employees to dedicate 20% of their time to side projects, fostering a culture of innovation and creativity (Google, n.d.). This approach has led to the development of successful products like Gmail and AdSense. (source: Google) https://www.google.ca/
25. Ed Catmull (September 2008). How Pixar Fosters Collective Creativity. Harvard Business Review.) https://hbr.org/2008/09/how-pixar-fosters-collective-creativity
26. The Canadian Space Agency (CSA) collaborates with academic institutions and private sector partners to foster innovation in space exploration and technology development (Canadian Space Agency, 2024). (Source: Canadian Space Agency, "Collaborative Initiatives"). https://www.asc-csa.gc.ca/eng/publications/dp-2024-2025.asp
27. Netflix's strategic shift from DVD rentals to streaming positioned it as a market leader (Netflix, 2007). Recognizing the evolving landscape and consumer preferences, the company capitalized on improving internet speeds to thrive in the burgeoning streaming market. (source: Netflix). https://www.netflix.com/
28. A case study by DataNext.ai highlights Coca-Cola's strategic decision to diversify its product portfolio beyond carbonated beverages. (Source: Coca-Cola's Strategic Shift, 2023) https://www.datanext.ai/case-study/coca-cola-non-soda-strategy
29. The Treasury Board of Canada Secretariat (TBS) implements strategic procurement practices, including competitive bidding processes and performance-based contracting. These initiatives aim to optimize government spending and ensure value for taxpayers. (Source: Treasury Board of Canada Secretariat, "Procurement Strategy" 2023). https://www.tbs-sct.canada.ca/pol/doc-eng.aspx?id=32692
30. Source: C. S. Dweck and K. Hogan, "How Microsoft Uses a Growth Mindset to Develop Leaders," Harvard Business Review, Oct. 2016. Leadership Development: Microsoft has developed leadership principles that encourage managers to model, coach, and care. This framework emphasizes the importance of being a role model, staying curious, and genuinely caring about colleagues.
31. Employee Engagement: Microsoft uses interactive online modules, storytelling, and various engagement tools like games and quizzes to promote growth mindset behaviors among employees. Growth Mindset and Coaching Culture at Microsoft.
32. Continuous Learning: The company rewards employees for their growth mindset and curiosity, traits that are integral to driving business outcomes. Microsoft Viva Learning is an example of a platform that supports employees in their learning journey, offering

personalized recommendations and resources. Source: How Microsoft Overhauled Its Approach to Growth Mindset. NeuroLeadership Institute. (n.d.) https://neuroleadership.com/
33. Canada School of Public Service (CSPS). (n.d.). Coaching, Mentoring, and Networking Learning Path. https://www.csps-efpc.gc.ca/coach-mentor-network-eng.aspx
34. Generative Leadership in Canada's Public Sector" by the Boston Consulting Group (BCG). Published on November 21, 2022, it explores how Generative Leadership, a humanistic framework, fosters renewal and growth, particularly during periods of significant change. The article emphasizes leading with both the head and heart to create a culture where employees can excel, receive coaching, and be recognized for their contributions. https://www.bcg.com/publications/2022/generative-leadership-aiding-canadas-public-sector
35. A Guide to the Project Management Body of Knowledge (PMBOK® Guide). 7th Edition. Project Management Institute, 2021.
36. Kotter, John P. *Leading Change*. Harvard Business Review Press, 1996.
37. Hiatt, J. M. (2003). "ADKAR: A Model for Change." *Prosci Research*. Available at: Prosci ADKAR
38. Brown, T. (2009). Change by Design: How Design Thinking Creates New Alternatives for Business and Society. Harper Business. This book provides insights into how design thinking can transform organizations and is foundational to understanding Brown's approach.
39. GROW Model. Whitmore, J. (1992). Coaching for Performance: GROWing Human Potential and Purpose. Nicholas Brealey Publishing. United Kingdom.
40. Solution Focused Model. de Shazer, S., & Berg, I. K. (1994). Changing Conversations in Therapy: A Theory of Solution-Focused Brief Therapy. Jossey-Bass. USA.
41. GROWTH Mindset Model. Dweck, C. S. (2006). Mindset: The New Psychology of Success. Random House. USA.
42. McKinsey & Company. (2019). "The DARE framework: A new approach to decision-making in complex organizations." McKinsey Quarterly. Retrieved from McKinsey.com.
43. Little, Jason. Lean Change Management: Innovative Practices for Managing Organizational Change. Happy Melly Express, 2014. ISBN: 978-0990466505.
44. Gama, João. Panoptic Model: A Comprehensive Approach to Managing Organizational Change, 2023.
45. McKinsey's "Inside-Out" Leadership Journey: How personal growth creates the path to success - This piece explores how personal growth and self-reflection are crucial for leaders to connect authentically with their teams and organizations. By Dana Maor, Hans-Werner Kaas, Kurt Strovink, and Ramesh Srinivasan. June 17, 2024 | Article

46. Ernst & Young's (EY) Coaching for Leaders - This resource outlines EY's approach to leadership coaching, focusing on embedding coaching into strategy to accelerate results and develop better leaders. Karen Hutchinson and Richard Skippon. EY Canada 2018
47. To Build a Culture of Experimentation, Start With Bad Ideas - How one company embraced experimentation to empower their employees. Joe Brown, October 2018. This article from IDEO discusses how embracing experimentation and learning from failures can foster a culture of innovation.
48. Know Your Customers' "Jobs to Be Done" - Is innovation inherently a hit-or-miss endeavor? Not if you understand why customers make the choices they make. by Clayton M. Christensen, Taddy Hall, Karen Dillon and David S. Duncan. From the Magazine (September 2016)
49. Kelley, David. "How to Move to a Culture of Experimentation Rather Than Planning." IDEO Insights. IDEO. www.ideo.com/insights.